WORLD WORD SEARCH

Toni Lynn Cloutier

STERLING CHILDREN'S BOOKS

New York

STERLING CHILDREN'S BOOKS
New York

An Imprint of Sterling Publishing
387 Park Avenue South
New York, NY 10016

Lot#:
2   4   6   8   10   9   7   5   3   1
06/11

Published by Sterling Publishing Co., Inc.
© 2011 by Toni Lynn Cloutier

Distributed in Canada by Sterling Publishing
c/o Canadian Manda Group, 165 Dufferin Street
Toronto, Ontario, Canada M6K 3H6
Distributed in the United Kingdom by GMC Distribution Services
Castle Place, 166 High Street, Lewes, East Sussex, England BN7 1XU
Distributed in Australia by Capricorn Link (Australia) Pty. Ltd.
P.O. Box 704, Windsor, NSW 2756, Australia

Illustrations by Adam Raiti

Manufactured in Canada

Sterling ISBN 978-1-4027-6906-1

For information about custom editions, special sales, premium and corporate purchases, please contact Sterling Special Sales Department at 800-805-5489 or specialsales@sterlingpublishing.com.

www.sterlingpublishing.com/kids

CONTENTS

INTRODUCTION 7

PUZZLES 8

Africa 8

Antarctica 18

Asia 20

Australia 48

Europe 50

North America 78

South America 96

ANSWERS 108

INTRODUCTION

Welcome to *World Word Search*, where you will discover lots of cool facts about the seven continents and the many countries that make up planet Earth.

Each puzzle is designed in the shape of a country or continent. The name of the countries' capitals are located in the puzzles where you would find the capitals on a map. (The first letter of the capital's name marks the spot.) The capitalized words in bold lettering in the text are the words hidden within each puzzle. Words may be hidden forward, backward, up, down, or in any of the diagonal directions. When searching for a word, ignore all spaces, accents, and punctuation. For example, if you are looking for "CÔTE D'IVOIRE" in the grid, you need to find "COTEDIVOIRE." Commas separate words for you to find. For example, if you see "ANGOLA, ETHIOPIA, LIBERIA," you need to find three different words.

You'll find facts such as each country's capital and currency, the Seven Wonders of the World, and much more. There are even questions to test your knowledge as you go. (The answers appear upside-down at the bottom of each word bank.)

So grab a pencil and take a fact-filled journey around the globe!

—Toni Lynn Cloutier

AFRICA

Africa is made up of 54 independent countries, including **ALGERIA**, **ANGOLA**, **ETHIOPIA**, **LIBERIA**, **MOROCCO**, **NIGER**, **RWANDA**, and ~~**SOMALIA.**~~

BENIN was called The Republic of Dahomey from 1960 to 1975.

BURKINA FASO means "Land of the Honest People."

BURUNDI was once called Ruanda-Urundi, because it was once part of two kingdoms.

Animals such as antelope, gorillas, and lions live in the **CENTRAL AFRICAN** Republic.

The **COMOROS** are a group of islands in the Indian Ocean.

The Republic of **CÔTE D'IVOIRE** is also known as the Ivory Coast.

Lowest point: Lake Assal, in **DJIBOUTI**, is 509 feet below sea level.

EGYPT is home to two of the Seven Wonders of the Ancient World: the Pyramids of Giza and the Lighthouse of Alexandria.

The equator runs through the upper half of **GABON**.

After finding a 10-million-year-old humanoid jawbone fragment in **KENYA**, anthropologists believe that Africa is the birthplace of human beings.

LAKE TANGANYIKA is the world's longest freshwater lake.

MADAGASCAR is the world's fourth largest island.

The country of **MAURITIUS** is an island in the Indian Ocean.

NIGERIA is Africa's most populous country.

At approximately 11,684,000 square miles, Africa is the world's **SECOND** largest continent.

The island nation of **SEYCHELLES** is Africa's smallest country.

SIERRA LEONE is one of the world's largest producers of diamonds.

In 1991, Nelson Mandela became the first black president of **SOUTH AFRICA**.

SUDAN is Africa's largest country.

Highest point: Mount Kilimanjaro in **TANZANIA**, at 19,340 feet

Victoria Falls waterfall lies between **ZAMBIA** and **ZIMBABWE**.

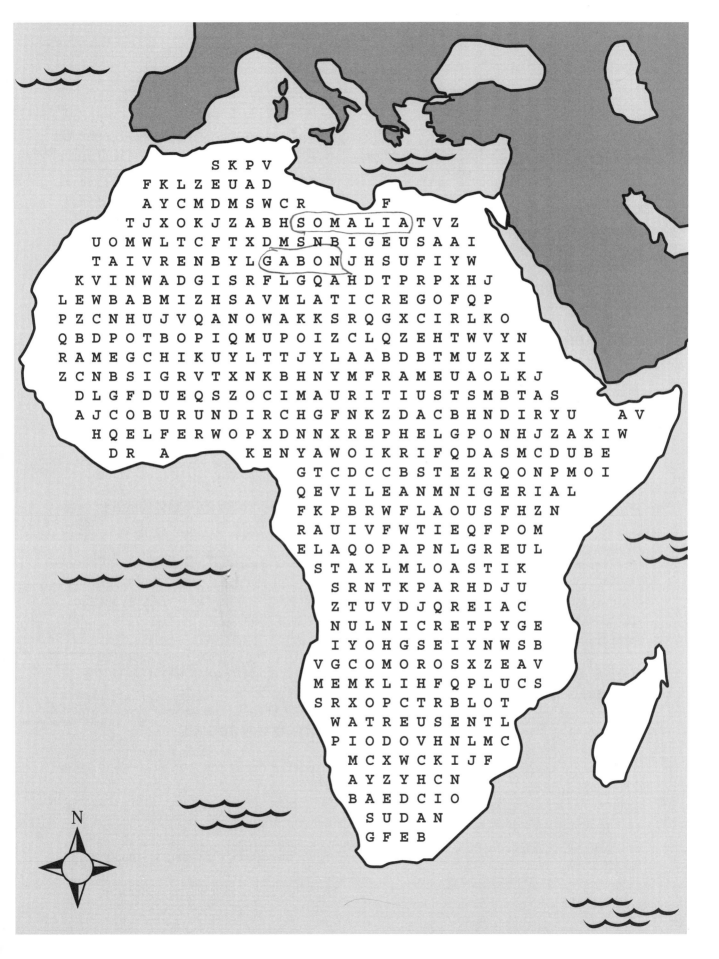

EGYPT

Alexander the Great founded **ALEXANDRIA** in 331 BCE. It is Egypt's second largest city.

CAIRO is Egypt's capital and Africa's largest city.

The **DUGONG** is a rare herbivore that resembles a manatee; it lives in the Red Sea.

A **GALABIYYA** is a long shirtlike garment worn by a man.

Egypt created the world's first national **GOVERNMENT**, as well as **MATHEMATICS**, **WRITING**, and the 365-day **CALENDAR**.

Developed in Egypt, **HIEROGLYPHICS** are a form of picture writing.

Highest point: **JABAL KATRINAH**, at 8,651 feet

Official name: **JUMHURIYAT MISR AL-ARABIYAH**, meaning "Arab Republic of Egypt."

A **KHAMSIN** is a hot dry wind occurring during the months of April and May, blowing dust and sand, and blocking out the sun.

A suq is an outdoor **MARKETPLACE**.

Egyptians' water supply and crops rely on the **NILE**, the world's longest river, and Lake Nasser, created by the **ASWAN HIGH DAM**.

Egyptians made **PAPYRUS**, the world's first paperlike writing material, from papyrus plants.

Currency: Egyptian **POUND**

A **PYRAMID** is a tomb made for a ruler.

Lake **QAROUN** is Egypt's largest saltwater lake.

Lowest point: **QATTARA** Depression, at 436 feet below sea level

RAS MOHAMED is one of Egypt's oldest national parks.

*The **RED SEA** separates Egypt from which peninsula?*

Government: **REPUBLIC** (headed by a president)

Located in Giza, **THE GREAT SPHINX** has the head of a man and the body, feet, and tail of a lion. *Do you know what it's made of?*

Egypt is the **THIRD** most populous country in Africa.

Egypt gained its independence from the **UNITED KINGDOM** in 1922.

Egyptian dress for a woman includes a **VEIL**.

(The Great Sphinx is made of: **Limestone**)

(Peninsula separated from Egypt by the Red Sea: **Arabian**)

ETHIOPIA

Ethiopia's original name was **ABYSSINIA**.

Capital: **ADDIS ABABA**

Official language: **AMHARIC**

Currency: Ethiopian **BIRR**

Similar in size to Niagara Falls, the **BLUE NILE FALLS** are 1,312 feet wide and drop 150 feet.

The Ethiopian **BUSH CROW** and the Prince Ruspoli's **TURACO** are 2 of 16 common birds found in Ethiopia.

Gondar is home to **CASTLES** that were built between 1632 and 1855.

The **DANAKIL DEPRESSION** is one of the world's hottest places.

GENNA, a game similar to hockey, is played each Lidet (Christmas) on January 7.

Some of the earliest-known human remains have been found in the **GREAT RIFT VALLEY**.

INJERA is a large piece of flat bread made from flour.

LAKE TANA is Ethiopia's largest lake.

In 1974, Donald Johanson discovered a hominid skeleton dating back 3.5 million years, in Hadar. He named it **LUCY**.

A **MARESHA** is an old wooden plow that farmers still use today.

Government: Federal **PARLIAMENTARY** Assembly (headed by a prime minister)

Highest point: **RAS DASHEN TERARA**, at 15,158 feet

Official name: Federal Democratic **REPUBLIC** of Ethiopia.

Located in Aksum, the Cathedral of **SAINT MARY** in Zion is considered Ethiopia's most sacred shrine.

A **SHAMMA** is a white, one-piece cotton cloth worn by men and women.

Located in Bale, the **SOF OMAR CAVE** System was carved out by the Wey River.

Ethiopia has **TWO SEASONS**. The dry season is from October to May, and the wet season is from June to September.

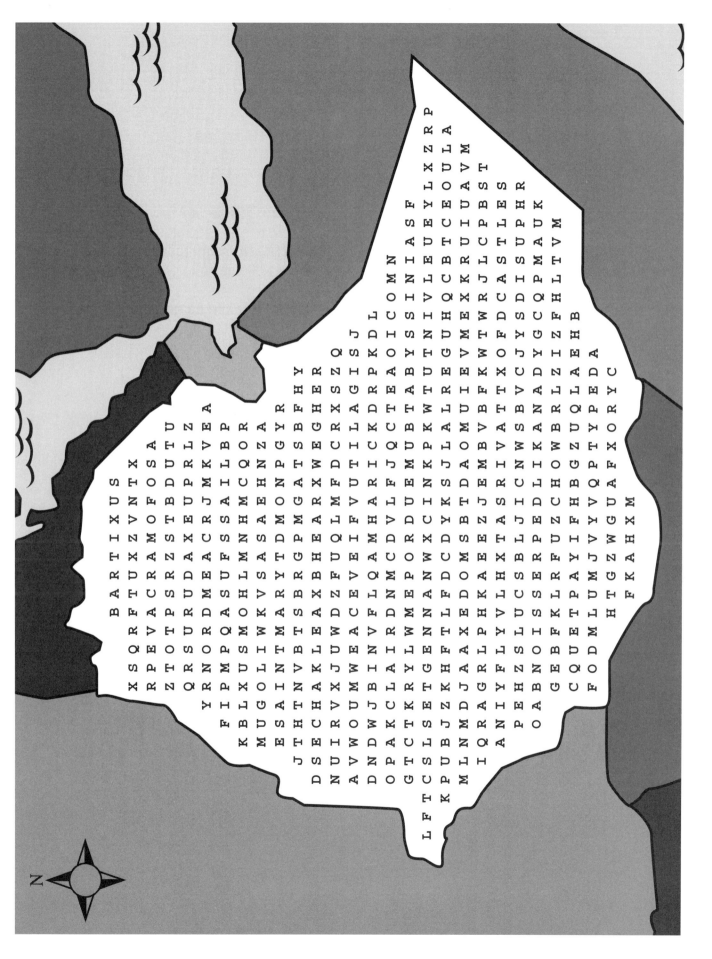

KENYA

ATHI and **TANA** are Kenya's two main rivers.

CAPE GOOSEBERRY is a plant that grows edible, tart berries.

DANCING is a popular recreational activity throughout the country.

Rural homes are made of straw roofs, mud walls, and **DIRT FLOORS**.

The large common antelope called **ELAND** can be found here.

ELEPHANTS, ZEBRAS, and many other animals roam throughout open fields here.

Official languages: **ENGLISH** and **SWAHILI**

The **EQUATOR** runs through the middle of Kenya.

The **FOSSIL** skeleton of a 12-year-old boy who lived 400,000 years ago was found here in 1984.

Official name: **JAMHURI YA KENYA**, meaning "Republic of Kenya."

Currency: **KENYAN SHILLING**

Africa's highest mountain, **KILIMANJARO**, *borders Kenya and which other country?*

LAKE VICTORIA is Africa's largest lake.

MAIZE (corn) is an important crop in Kenya.

A **MATATU** is the name for a minibus.

MOMBASA is Kenya's second largest city.

Highest point: **MOUNT KENYA**, at 17,058 feet

Capital: **NAIROBI**

PASTORALISTS are people who move from place to place and raise livestock for a living.

Government: **REPUBLIC** (headed by cabinet ministers)

Kenya gained its independence from the **UNITED KINGDOM** in 1963.

Each June, the **WILDEBEEST** gather at the Masai Mara National Reserve to give birth.

(Other country bordering Mount Kilimanjaro: **Tanzania**)

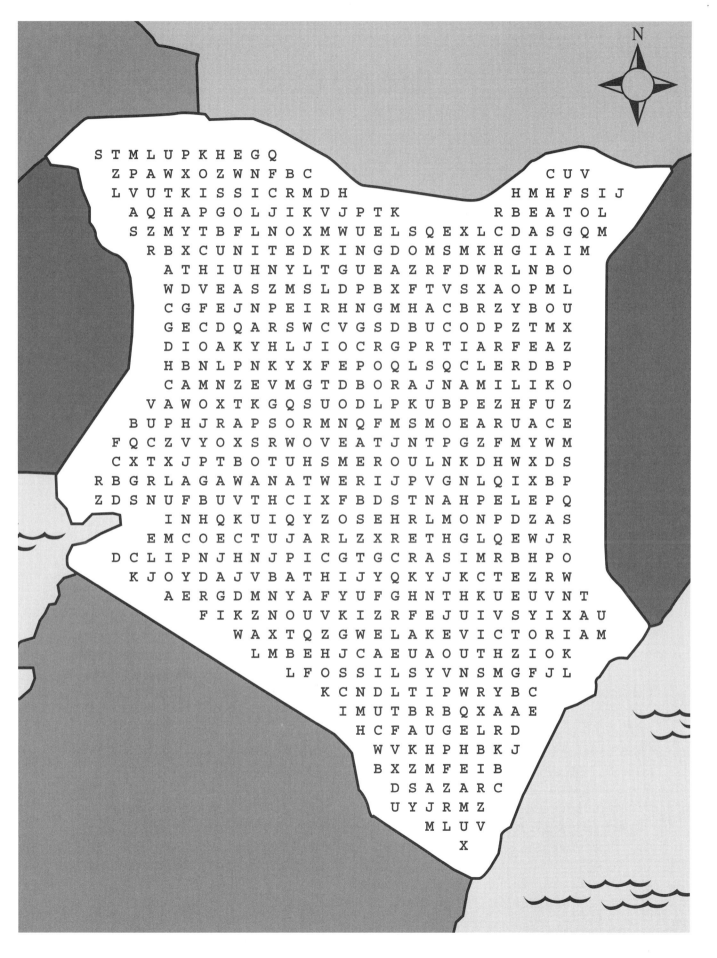

MOROCCO

Founded in 859, the University of **AL-KARAOUINE** is the one of the world's oldest educational institutions.

Official language: **ARABIC**

The population of Morocco includes **ARABS** and **BERBERS**.

The **ATLAS** Mountains are a chain of mountains that runs through the middle of the country, from southwest to northeast.

Many urban homes are built with flattened tin cans called **BIDONS**.

CASABLANCA is Morocco's largest city.

COUSCOUS is a national dish made of steamed wheat, vegetables, fish or meat, and a thin sauce.

Currency: Moroccan **DIRHAM**

Morocco catches the most **FISH** of any African country.

*The Strait of **GIBRALTAR** separates Morocco from which other country?*

At 689 feet high, the **HASSAN II MOSQUE** in Casablanca is the world's tallest, and third largest, mosque.

The first Moroccan state was led by **IDRIS IBN ABD ALLAH** in the late 700s.

Official religion: **ISLAM**

Highest point: **JEBEL TOUBKAL**, at 13,665 feet

A **JELLABA** is a loose-fitting, long-sleeved hooded robe worn by a man.

A suq is an outdoor **MARKET**, also used as a weekly gathering place.

National drink: **MINT TEA**

Located in Rabat, the **MOHAMMED V** University is Morocco's largest university.

Government: Constitutional **MONARCHY** (headed by a king)

Many countryside homes have **ONE LARGE ROOM** in which people cook, sleep, and live.

Morocco exports much of the **PHOSPHATE** used throughout the world.

At times throughout its history, the city of Asilah has been home to many **PIRATES**.

Capital: **RABAT**

Pirate Pasha Raissouni built the **RAISSOUNI** Palace.

The **SAHARA** is the world's largest desert; it stretches across part of Morocco.

(Country separated from Morocco by the Strait of Gibraltar: **Spain**)

16

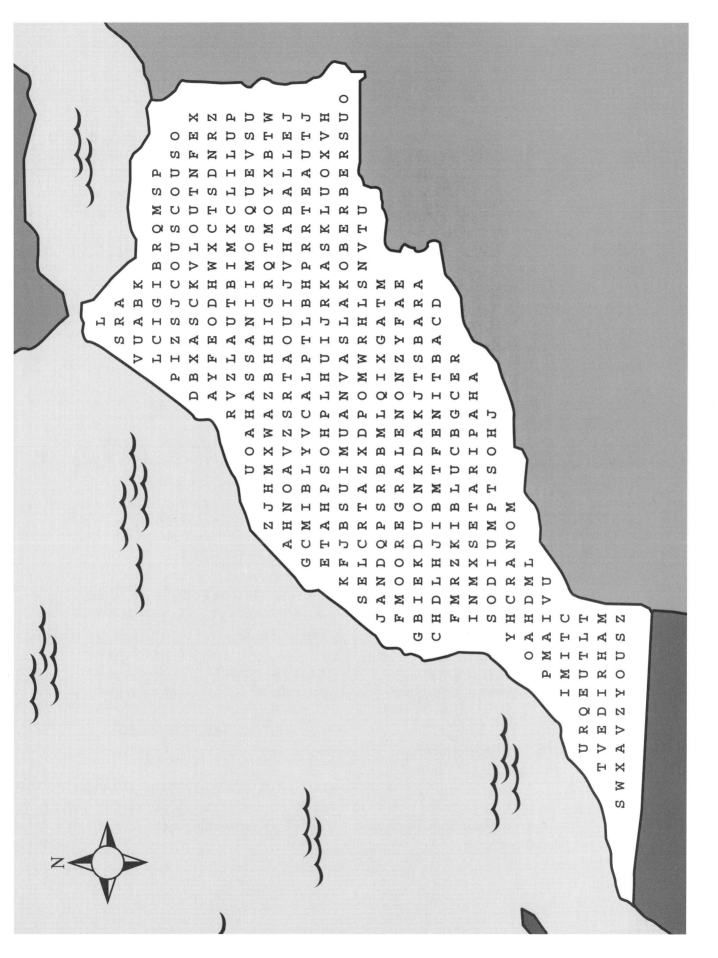

ANTARCTICA

The **ANTARCTIC TREATY** states that Antarctica is to be used for research and peaceful purposes.

CALVING is when the outer edge of an ice shelf breaks away and forms an iceberg.

Antarctica lies in the center of the Antarctic **CIRCLE**.

Antarctica is the world's **COLDEST** region.

There are no **CROWS** in Antarctica.

With no rain and only about two inches of snow each year, Antarctica has the Earth's **DRIEST** climate.

EAST ANTARCTICA has the thickest ice on the continent, and makes up more than half of Antarctica.

At approximately 5,400,000 square miles, Antarctica is the world's **FIFTH** largest continent in surface area.

The continent is made of the East Antarctica and the West Antarctica **ICE SHEETS**.

An **ICE SHELF** is a flat platform of floating ice that is still attached to land.

ICEBREAKERS are large ships that plow through the ice to get supplies to people who live in Antarctica.

KRILL are shrimplike animals that are a major food source for other water animals.

Similar to a fly, the half-inch-long wingless **MIDGE** is Antarctica's largest land animal.

MOSSES are Antarctica's most common plants.

MOUNT EREBUS is Antarctica's most active volcano.

PLANT FOSSILS reveal that the continent once had a warm, ice-free climate with trees and leafy plant life.

The **ROSS ICE SHELF** is Antarctica's largest ice shelf. The center is 2,300 feet thick, and the outer edge is 660 feet thick.

SEA ICE forms in the winter when the Southern Ocean surface freezes into sheets of salty ice.

The **SOUTH POLE** lies close to the center of Antarctica. *Where is the North Pole located?*

The **TRANSANTARCTIC** Mountains separate Antarctica's two ice sheets.

Highest point: **VINSON MASSIF**, at 16,067 feet

On July 21, 1983, **VOSTOK STATION** recorded the world's lowest temperature at −128.6 degrees Fahrenheit.

(Where the North Pole is located: **the center of the Arctic Ocean**)

ASIA

AZERBAIJAN and **IRAN** border the world's largest inland body of water, the Caspian Sea.

BAHRAIN is an island country in the Persian Gulf.

The Brahmaputra River flows through **BANGLADESH** and **INDIA** and then connects to the Ganges River.

Asia is made up of about 50 countries, including **BHUTAN**, **CAMBODIA**, **JORDAN**, and **SYRIA**.

BRUNEI, INDONESIA, and **MALAYSIA** each have part of the world's third largest island, Borneo. *What are the world's two largest islands?*

CHINA has the largest population in the world.

CYPRUS is an island country in the Mediterranean Sea.

The **DEAD SEA** is the world's saltiest body of water.

IRAQ is home to one of the Seven Wonders of the Ancient World, The Hanging Gardens of Babylon.

The East Sea, or the Sea of Japan, separates **JAPAN** from **NORTH KOREA** and **SOUTH KOREA**.

KUWAIT, OMAN, QATAR, SAUDI ARABIA, UNITED ARAB EMIRATES, and **YEMEN** are all located in the Arabian Desert.

KYRGYZSTAN, TAJIKISTAN, and **UZBEKISTAN** gained independence in 1991 when the USSR officially disbanded.

LAOS gained its full independence from France in 1953.

At approximately 17,139,000 square miles, Asia is the world's **LARGEST** continent in surface area.

MALDIVES is Asia's smallest independent country.

Mount Everest, the highest place on Earth, is located on the border of **NEPAL** and Tibet.

Only 1,000 of the 7,000 islands that make up the **PHILIPPINES** are populated.

The Johor Strait separates **SINGAPORE** from Malaysia.

TAIWAN is an island in the South China Sea.

TURKEY is home to three of the Seven Wonders of the Ancient World: the Temple of Artemis at Ephesus, the Haga Sophia at Istanbul, and the Mausoleum at Halicarnassus.

The Karakum Desert covers 135,000 square miles of **TURKMENISTAN**.

(World's two largest islands: Greenland, New Guinea)

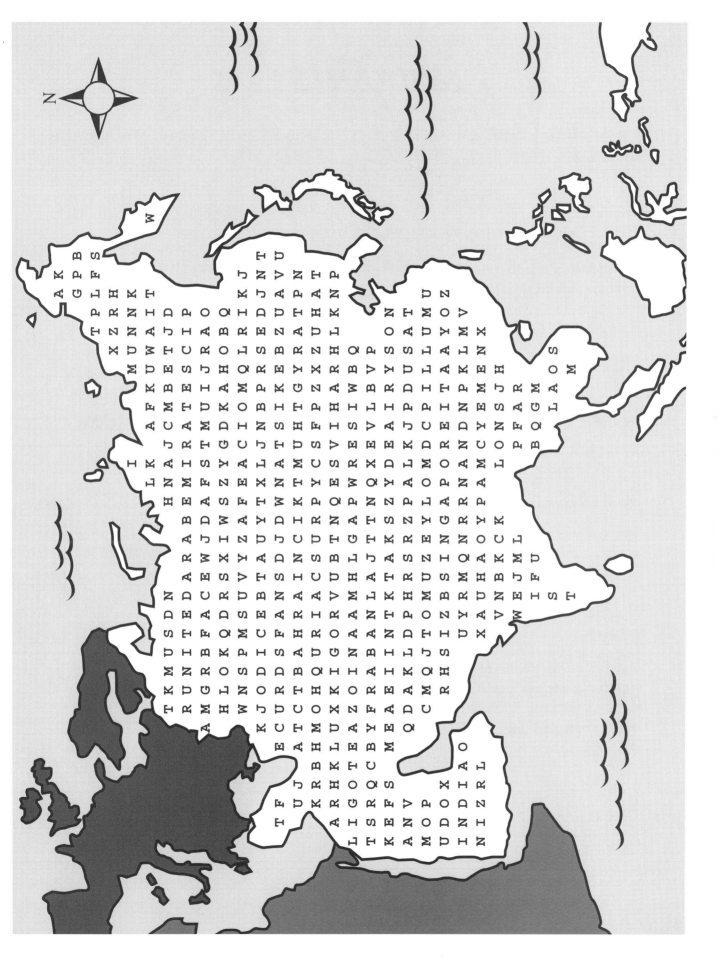

AFGHANISTAN

The **AFGHAN HOUND** is used to protect sheep from wolves.

Currency: Afghanistan **AFGHANI**

The **ATTAN** is a popular folk dance here.

A **BURQA** is a long, hooded garment worn by Pashtun women.

National sport: **BUZKASHI**

CRICKET is a popular sport in Afghanistan.

DOGH is a drink made of yogurt, cold water, cucumber, salt, and dried mint.

People who travel from place to place usually live in tents made of **GOAT HAIR**.

The **HINDU KUSH** Mountains are located in the central highlands, where many Afghans live in valleys.

Official name and government: **ISLAMIC REPUBLIC** of Afghanistan (headed by a president)

Capital: **KABUL**

The **KHYBER PASS** links Afghanistan to Pakistan.

LAPIS LAZULI is a deep blue, valuable stone found here.

The **LEOPARD BANE** plant is used to treat snakebites and scorpion stings.

Rural people live in homes made of sun-dried **MUD BRICKS**.

A **MULLAH** is a religious leader in a village or nomadic group.

There are **NO RAILROADS** in Afghanistan.

People who move from place to place with their goat or sheep herds are known as **NOMADS**.

Highest point: **NOWSHAK**, at 24,557 feet

Official languages: **PASHTO** and **DARI**

The **SANTOLIN YARROW** plant is used to ease headaches and toothaches.

Whole-grain **SOURDOUGH** bread is served with almost every meal.

Some people eat the bulb of a Cilician **TULIP** for strength.

Afghanistan gained its independence from the **UNITED KINGDOM** in 1919.

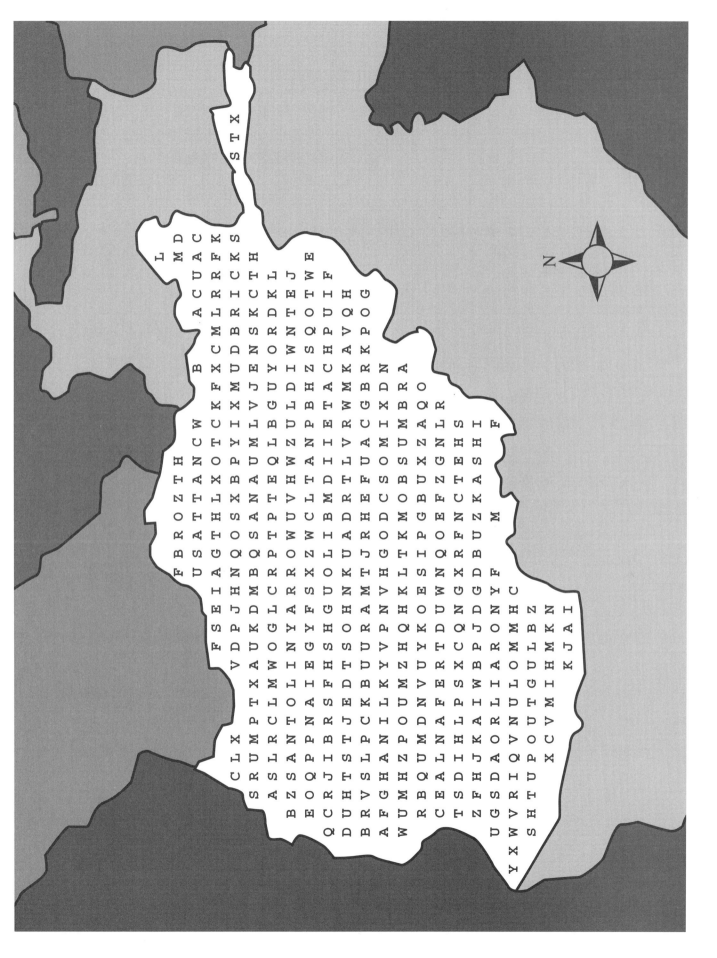

CHINA

Capital: **BEIJING**

BUDDHISM is a popular religion in China.

Chinese **CALLIGRAPHY** is a form of writing that uses a brush.

Government: Chinese **COMMUNIST PARTY** (headed by a state council)

Official name: Zhonghua Renmin **GONGHEGUO**, meaning "People's Republic of China."

In 1997, **HONG KONG** became part of China.

The **INDUS RIVER** *flows through China and which other two countries?*

MONSOONS are winds that cause the seasons to change.

At 29,035 feet, **MOUNT EVEREST** is the world's highest mountain and China's highest point.

Official language: **NORTHERN CHINESE**. It is also called Mandarin and Putonghua in Chinese.

PAPER was invented here in 105 CE.

China has the largest **POPULATION** of any country in the world.

Currency: **RENMINBI**, or Yuan

SHANGHAI is China's largest city, and one of the world's largest cities.

TAI CHI is a popular exercise.

TAIWAN is an island located in the South China Sea.

TAKLIMAKAN is one of the world's driest deserts.

TAOISM is a religion practiced here that teaches one to live in peace with nature.

China is the world's oldest country and **THIRD** largest country. *What is the world's largest country?*

The **THREE GORGES DAM** is the world's largest dam.

Lowest point: **TURPAN DEPRESSION**, at 505 feet

The world's highest town, **WENZHUAN**, is located here.

The **YANGTZE** is the world's third longest river. *Can you name the world's two longest rivers?*

(Longest rivers in the world: **Nile, in Africa; Amazon, in South America**)

(World's largest country: **Russia**)

(2 countries other than China through which the Indus River flows: **Pakistan and India**)

24

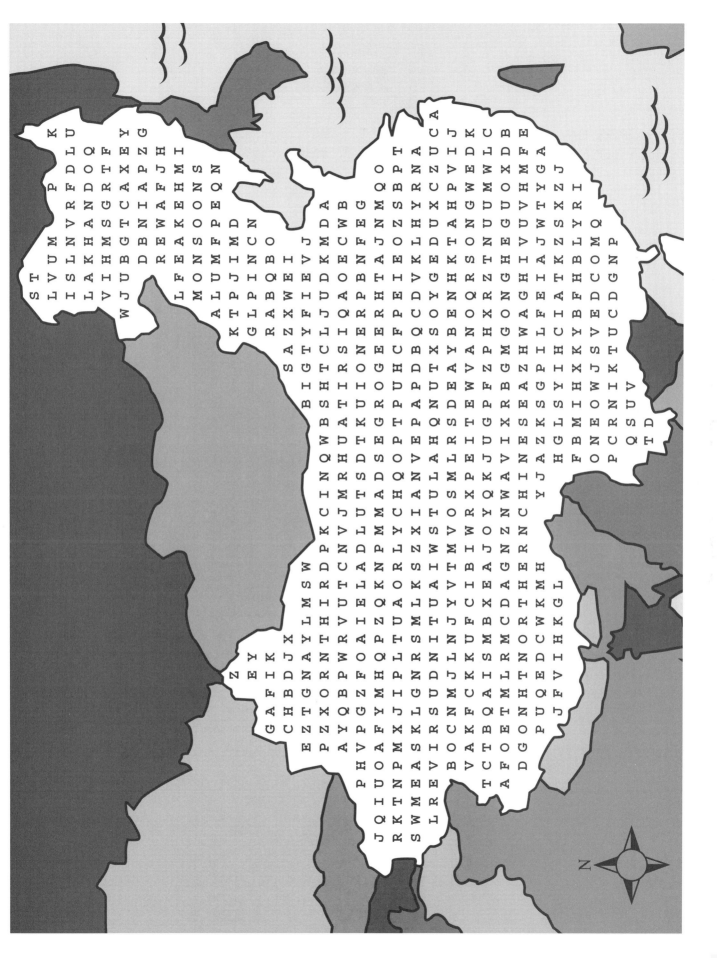

INDIA

BAILY Bridge is the world's highest bridge.

Official name: **BHARAT** Ganarajya, meaning "Republic of India."

India is the birthplace of the religion **BUDDHISM**.

The game **CHESS** was invented here.

CRICKET is India's most popular sport.

A **DHOTI** is a shirt-like wrap a man wears that drapes down past his waist.

Many people bathe in the **GANGES**, one of the world's longest rivers.

Located in northern India, the **HIMALAYAS** form the world's highest mountain system.

HOLI is a Hindu religious festival that celebrates the arrival of spring.

With over one million workers, **INDIAN RAILWAYS** employs more people than any other company in the world.

Currency: **INDIAN RUPEE**

Highest point: **KANCHENJUNGA**, at 28,208 feet

With over 1,000 **LANGUAGES**, India has more languages than any other country.

MUMBAI is India's largest city.

Capital: **NEW DELHI**

The world-famous book of five tales called the **PANCHATANTRA** originated in India.

There are more **POST OFFICES** in India than anywhere else on Earth.

Government: Federal **REPUBLIC** (headed by a prime minister)

SANSKRIT is India's oldest written language.

A **SARI** is a length of cloth that a woman wraps around her body.

India has the **SECOND** largest population of any country in the world. *Which country has the largest population?*

Himalaya means "House of **SNOW**" in Sanskrit.

Located in Agra, the **TAJ MAHAL** is India's most famous building.

(Country with the world's largest population: **China**)

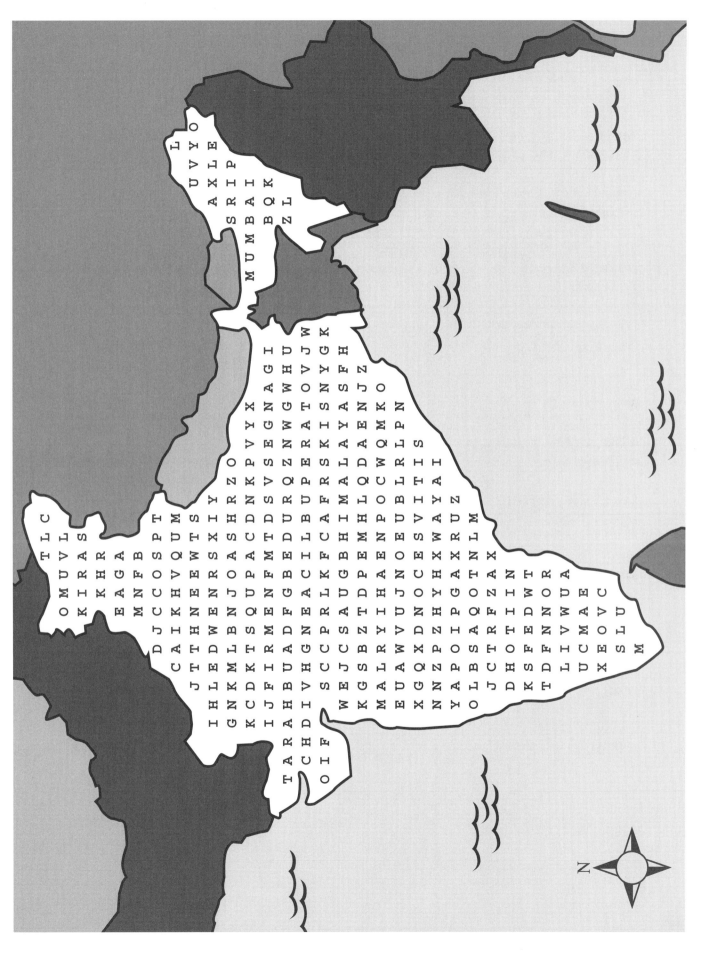

IRAN

Iran is a littler bigger in area than **ALASKA** in the United States.

Lowest point: **CASPIAN SEA**, at 92 feet below sea level

Iranians fish for sturgeon; their eggs are used to make a salty delicacy called **CAVIAR**.

The **DASHT-E-KAVIR** is also called the Great Salt Desert.

The **DASHT-E-LUT** is also called the Great Sand Desert.

A **DOLMEH** is a vegetable filled with meat and rice.

The **ELBURZ MOUNTAINS** stretch across the country from east to west.

A **FAQIH** is an Islamic religious leader.

Official language: **FARSI**

Currency: **IRANIAN RIAL**

Official name: **JOMHURI-YE ESLAMI-YE IRAN**, meaning "Islamic Republic of Iran."

A Muslim house of worship is called a **MOSQUE**.

Highest point: **MOUNT DAMAVAND**, at 18,386 feet

NOWRUZ is the Iranian New Year's Day, when they celebrate the spring equinox on March 21.

Iran was known as **PERSIA**, when leaders including Cyrus the Great and Xerxes ruled the country.

Iran is one of the world's leading producers of **PETROLEUM**.

Half of Iran consists of high, flat land called **PLATEAUS**.

The Persians created a **PONY EXPRESS** mail delivery system around 500 BCE.

Government: Islamic **REPUBLIC** (headed by a president)

Before 1979, Iran was ruled by a king, known as a **SHAH**.

Capital: **TEHRAN**

The **ZAGROS** Mountains border Iraq in the west.

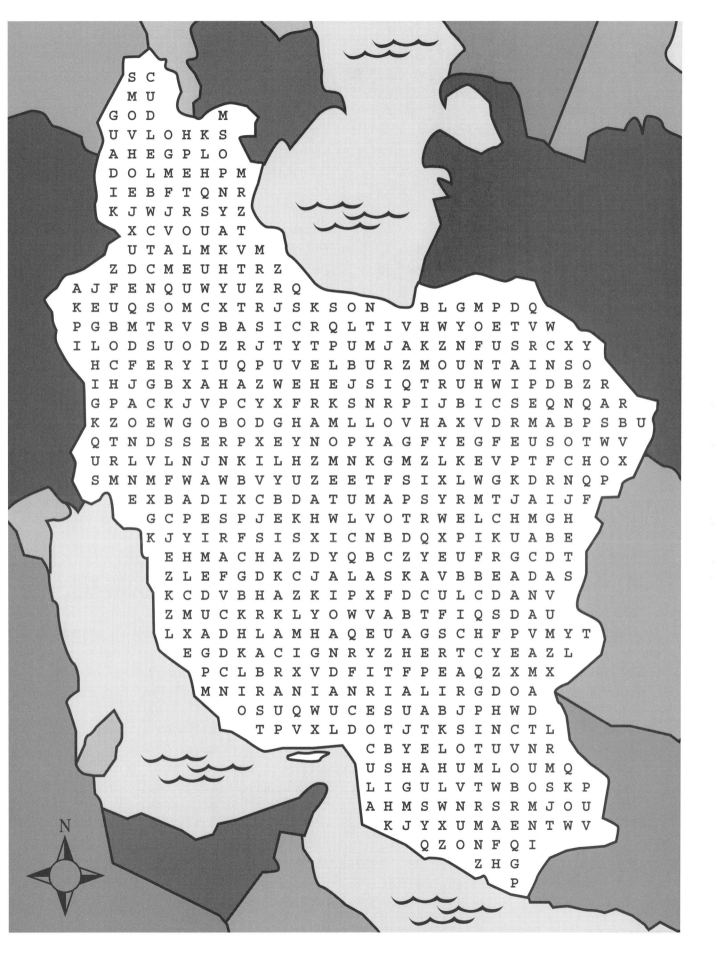

IRAQ

Offical languages: **ARABIC** and **KURDISH**

Northern Iraq was once known as **ASSYRIA**.

Alexander the Great once ruled **BABYLONIA**, which is now known as southern Iraq.

Capital: **BAGHDAD**

BARLEY and **WHEAT** are two of Iraq's major crops.

The world's first **CIVILIZATION** is believed to have developed in Mesopotamia.

DATES are a popular fruit. They grow on palm trees and are very sweet.

The **EUPHRATES** and the **TIGRIS** are Iraq's two major rivers.

Government: **FEDERAL REPUBLIC** (headed by a prime minister)

Ur was one of the world's **FIRST CITIES**.

Iraq is composed of 18 **GOVERNORATES**, or provinces.

Currency: **IRAQI DINAR**

Iraq was once called **MESOPOTAMIA**. Mesopotamia is a Greek word meaning "Land Between the Rivers."

MOSUL is one of Iraq's largest cities.

MUSLIN, a white cloth made from cotton yarn, was first made here.

Iraq's main energy sources are oil and **NATURAL GAS**.

NINEVEH was the last capital of the Assyrian Empire.

Official name: **REPUBLIC OF IRAQ**

SAMBUSAK is a traditional meal of moon-shaped dough, stuffed with meat or cheese.

SHATT AL-ARAB is a river formed where Iraq's two major rivers combine.

SOAP made from wood ash and animal fat was invented here.

A **STYLUS** is a stick people used to write on clay tablets in ancient times.

Some of the world's first cities were built in **SUMER**.

SUNDIALS were invented here.

The **SYRIAN DESERT** stretches along southwest and western Iraq.

WADIS are dry valleys in the desert that turn into rivers after it rains.

Highest point: **ZAGROS** Mountain, at 11,840 feet

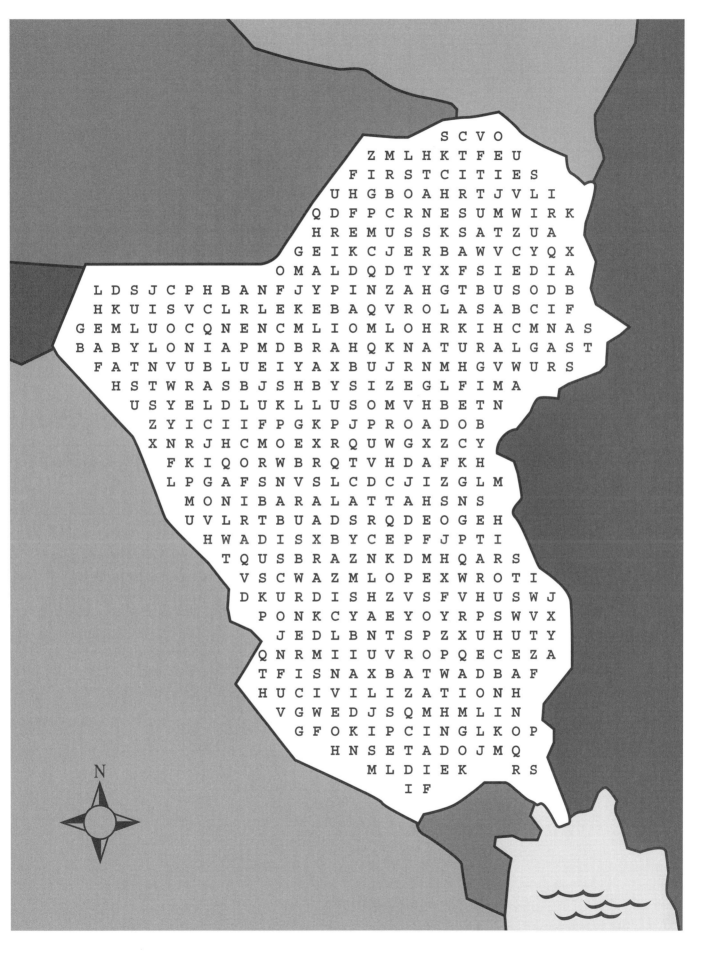

ISRAEL

Official languages: **ARABIC** and **HEBREW**

Israel's government uses **BASIC LAWS**. It has no written constitution.

David **BEN-GURION** (served 1948-1953, 1955-1963) was Israel's first Prime Minister.

Lowest point: The **DEAD SEA**, at 1,381 feet below sea level.

DIAMOND cutting is a profitable industry here.

A **DREIDEL** is a four-sided top that you spin. Playing with a dreidel is a tradition during the holiday of Hannukah.

FALAFEL are spicy, deep-fried balls of ground chickpeas or fava beans.

JAFFA is one of the oldest cities in the world.

Capital: **JERUSALEM**

Founded in 1948, the country is a homeland for the **JEWISH** people.

The **JORDAN** River is Israel's longest river.

The **KNESSET** is the name of Israel's parliament.

KOSHER is a word used to describe food prepared according to Jewish dietary laws.

Highest point: Mount **MERON**, at 3,963 feet

Israel's driest region is the **NEGEV** Desert.

Currency: Israeli **NEW SHEKEL**

ORTHODOX Jews strictly adhere to laws and values presented in the Torah, the historic holy book of the Jewish people.

Government: Democratic **REPUBLIC** (headed by a prime minister)

SHABBAT, the Jewish sabbath, begins Friday evening, when two candles are lit.

TEL AVIV is Israel's second largest city.

Chaim **WEIZMANN** (served 1949-1952) was Israel's first president.

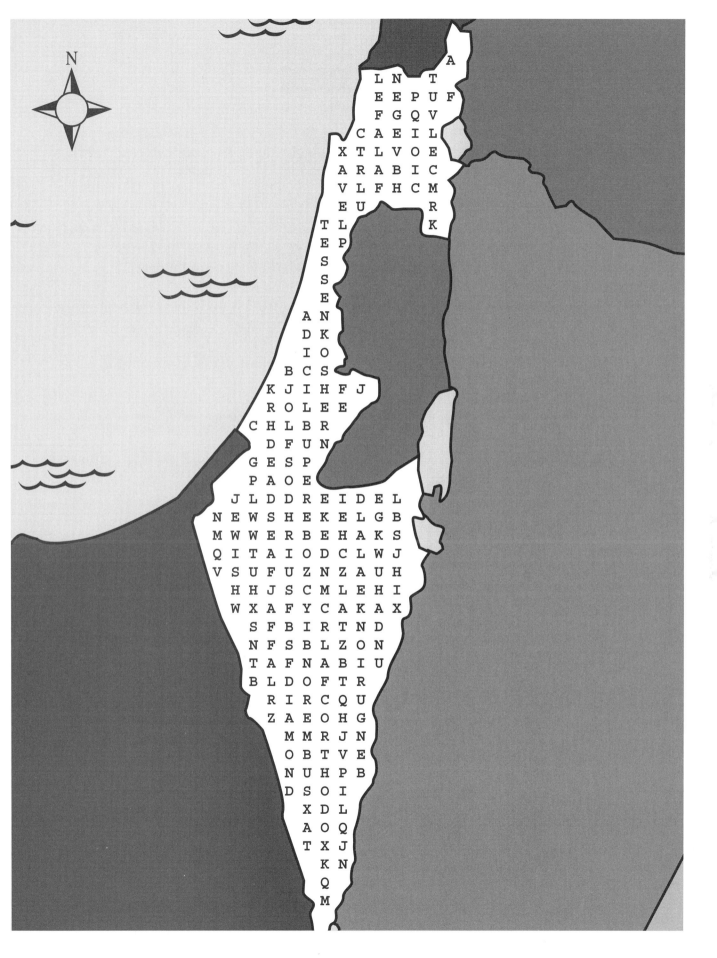

JAPAN

BEI-GOMA is a popular game in which each child spins a top, and the child with the last spinning top wins.

Highest point: Mount **FUJI**, at 12,388 feet

A **FURO** is a bath used for relaxing.

A **GENKAN** is the entryway to a home where people take off their shoes.

GOHAN means "meal" in Japanese.

HONSHU, Hokkaido, Kyushu, and Shikoku are Japan's four largest islands.

Official language: **JAPANESE**

Currency: **JAPANESE YEN**

Similar to fencing, **KENDO** is a sport in which you strike your opponent with a wooden stick in one of four strike zones for a point.

Government: Constitutional **MONARCHY** with a parliamentary government (headed by a prime minister)

White **RICE** is an important part of the Japanese diet.

SUMO wrestling is an ancient Japanese sport.

Capital: **TOKYO**

On March 14, **WHITE DAY**, a man gives marshmallow candy to a woman to express his love.

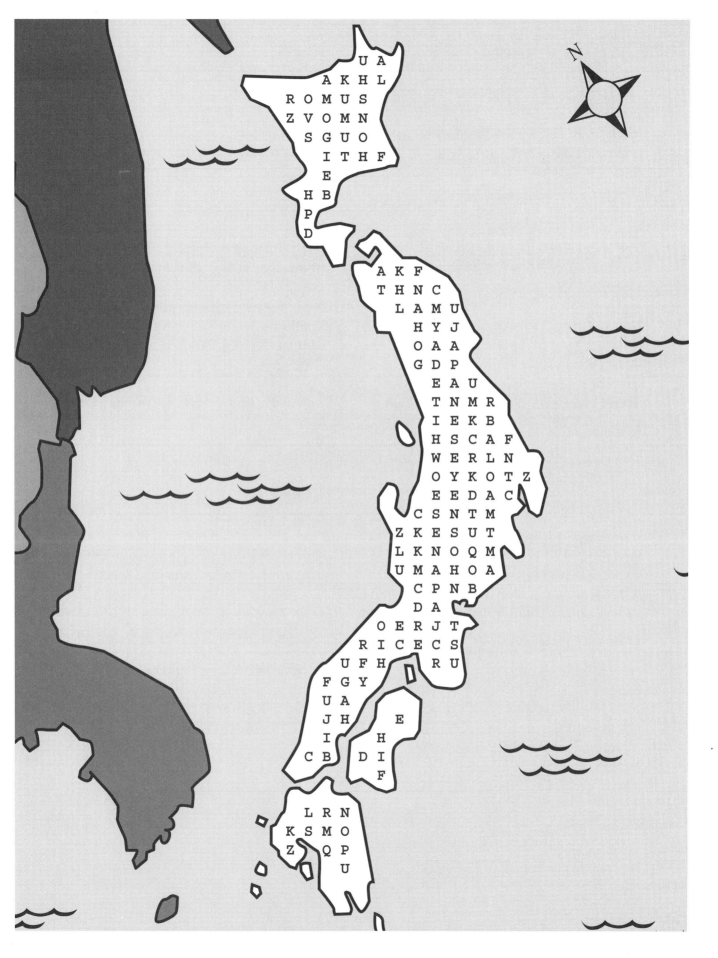

KOREA

In 1945, Korea was divided into two countries, **NORTH** Korea and **SOUTH** Korea.

CHEJU is South Korea's largest island.

The **CHUSEOK** festival takes place in October in celebration of the Harvest Moon.

North Korean government: **COMMUNIST** (headed by a State Administrative Council)

South Korea's highest point: **HALLA** Mountain, at 6,398 feet

The **HAN RIVER** flows through South Korea's capital, Seoul.

Invented in 1446, the **HAN'GUL** is the name of the Korean alphabet. It has 10 vowels and 14 consonants.

KIMCHI is a popular dish made of white radish and cabbage or other vegetables.

Korea's official language: **KOREAN**

Currency: North or South **KOREAN WON**

Located in South Korea, **LOTTE WORLD** includes the world's largest indoor theme park.

National flower of South Korea: **MUGUNGHWA** (*Hybiscus syriacus*)

At 325 miles long, **NAKTONG** is South Korea's longest river.

North Korea's highest point: **PAEKTU** Mountains, at 9,003 feet

North Korea's official name: Choson-Minjujuui-Inmin-Konghwaguk, meaning "Democratic **PEOPLE'S** Republic of Korea"

Capital of North Korea: **PYONGYANG**

South Korean government: **REPUBLIC** (headed by a prime minister)

The **SEA OF JAPAN** separates North Korea from Japan.

Capital of South Korea and one of the largest cities in the world: **SEOUL**

South Korea's official name: **TAEHAN-MIN'GUK**, meaning "Republic of Korea"

TAEKWONDO was invented here.

At 490 miles long, **YALU** is North Korea's longest river.

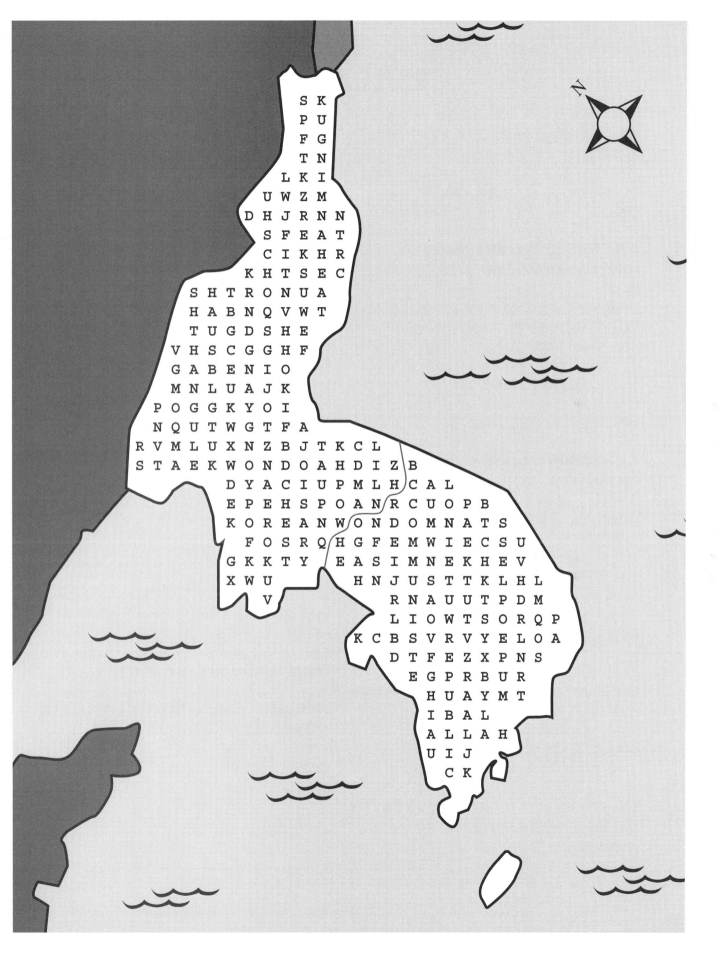

MALAYSIA

APA KHABAR means "How do you do?" in Malay.

Official language: **BAHASA** Malasia (Malay)

The South **CHINA SEA** separates Malaysia's two regions.

Malaysia is close to the earth's **EQUATOR**, causing the climate to be hot and humid.

National flower: **HIBISCUS**

Official religion: **ISLAM**

KAMPONGS are villages in rural areas where houses are made of bamboo.

Highest point: Mount **KINABALU**, at 13,431 feet

The **KOMPANG** is a hand drum that is used when celebrating special occasions.

Capital: **KUALA LUMPUR**

The **LION** dance is performed during the Chinese New Year in hopes of good fortune.

MALAYS, Chinese, and Indian are Malaysia's three major ethnic groups.

Government: Constitutional **MONARCHY** headed by a prime minister and parliament

NASI LEMAK is rice cooked in coconut milk, and is unofficially Malaysia's national dish.

PANTAI means "beach" in Malay.

Malaysia is divided into two regions. **PENINSULAR** Malaysia is the west part and has 11 states.

PERLIS is Malaysia's smallest state.

The **PETRONAS TOWERS** stand at 1,483 feet tall, making them two of the world's tallest skyscrapers.

PUTRAJAYA is home of the federal government.

The **RAFFLESIA PRICEI** is the world's largest flower; it grows in Borneo.

Currency: **RINGGIT**

A **SAPE** is a guitar-like instrument used by Indian tribes.

SARAWAK and **SABAH** are the only two states on the eastern half of Malaysia.

Men wear a traditional black hat called a **SONGKOK**.

TERIMA KASIH means "Thank you" in Malay.

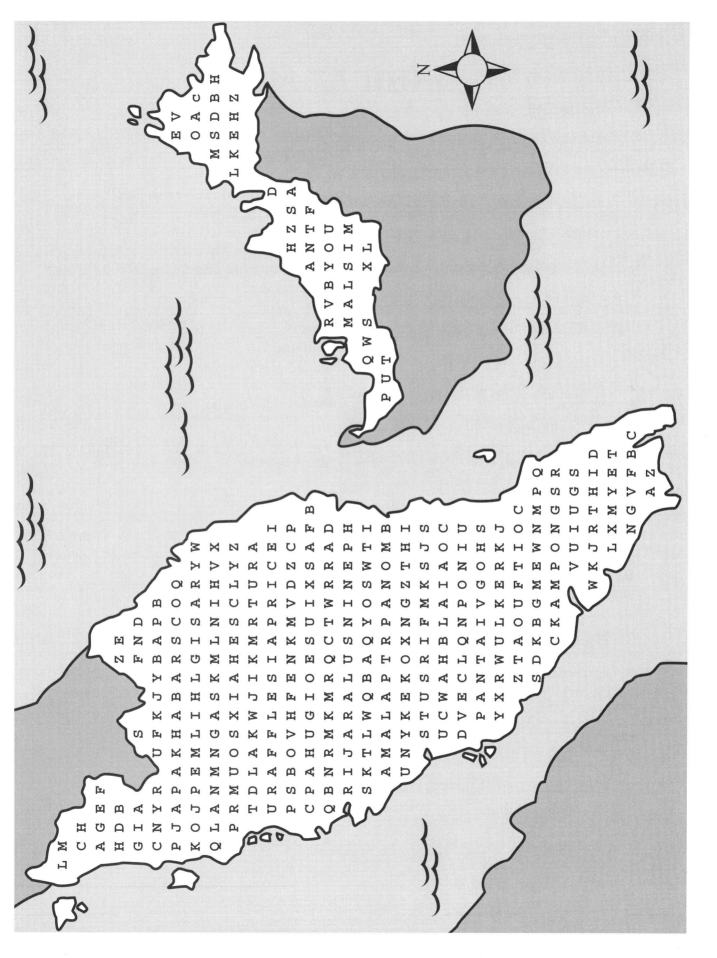

SAUDI ARABIA

ABHA receives the most rainfall in Saudi Arabia.

Official name: Al-Mamlaka Al-Arabiya **AL-SAUDIA**, meaning "Kingdom of Saudi Arabia."

Official language: **ARABIC**

ASIR is the southern part of the Western Highlands region where mountains rise over 9,000 feet.

Wadi **BISHA** Dam is Saudi Arabia's largest dam.

HEJAZ is the northern part of the Western Highlands region.

HORSE racing is a popular sporting event here.

IBEX, animals similar to mountain goats, can be found here.

The government is based on **ISLAMIC** law, and there is no written constitution.

Highest point: **JABAL SAWDA**, at 10,522 feet

JEDDAH is Saudi Arabia's second largest city.

KING SAUD University was established in 1957.

Saudi Arabia uses the **LUNAR CALENDAR**, which consists of 354 days.

MECCA is the holiest city for the Islamic religion and home to the shrine of **KAABA**.

Government: **MONARCHY** (headed by a king and a Council of Ministers)

Saudi Arabia is the world's leading **PETROLEUM** producer.

It is against the law to eat **PORK** in Saudi Arabia.

Capital: **RIYADH**

The **RUB AL-KHALI**, meaning "empty quarter" in Arabic, is one of the world's largest sand deserts.

Anthem: "**SAREI** Lil Majd Walaya"

Currency: **SAUDI RIYAL**

SOCCER is the country's most popular sport.

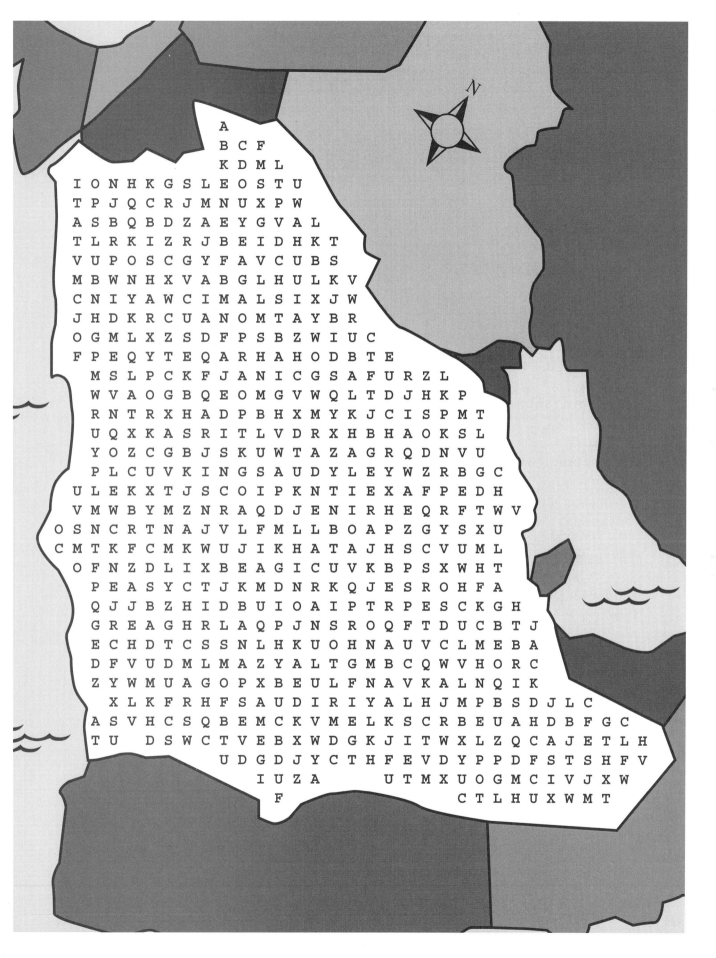

```
        A
        B C F
        K D M L
I O N H K G S L E O S T U
T P J Q C R J M N U X P W
A S B Q B D Z A E Y G V A L
T L R K I Z R J B E I D H K T
V U P O S C G Y F A V C U B S
M B W N H X V A B G L H U L K V
C N I Y A W C I M A L S I X J W
J H D K R C U A N O M T A Y B R
O G M L X Z S D F P S B Z W I U C
F P E Q Y T E Q A R H A H O D B T E
  M S L P C K F J A N I C G S A F U R Z L
  W V A O G B Q E O M G V W Q L T D J H K P
  R N T R X H A D P B H X M Y K J C I S P M T
  U Q X K A S R I T L V D R X H B H A O K S L
  Y O Z C G B J S K U W T A Z A G R Q D N V U
  P L C U V K I N G S A U D Y L E Y W Z R B G C
U L E K X T J S C O I P K N T I E X A F P E D H
V M W B Y M Z N R A Q D J E N I R H E Q R F T W V
O S N C R T N A J V L F M L L B O A P Z G Y S X U
C M T K F C M K W U J I K H A T A J H S C V U M L
O F N Z D L I X B E A G I C U V K B P S X W H T
P E A S Y C T J K M D N R K Q J E S R O H F A
Q J J B Z H I D B U I O A I P T R P E S C K G H
G R E A G H R L A Q P J N S R O Q F T D U C B T J
E C H D T C S S N L H K U O H N A U V C L M E B A
D F V U D M L M A Z Y A L T G M B C Q W V H O R C
Z Y W M U A G O P X B E U L F N A V K A L N Q I K
  X L K F R H F S A U D I R I Y A L H J M P B S D J L C
A S V H C S Q B E M C K V M E L K S C R B E U A H D B F G C
T U   D S W C T V E B X W D G K J I T W X L Z Q C A J E T L H
      U D G D J Y C T H F E V D Y P P D F S T S H F V
      I U Z A        U T M X U O G M C I V J X W
      F                C T L H U X W M T
```

TAIWAN

Oil from the **CAMPHOR** trees that grow here is used to make antiseptics and cosmetics.

Taiwan was Asia's first **CONSTITUTIONAL** republic.

Government: **DEMOCRATIC** (headed by a president)

During the **DONGGANG** King Boat Ritual, people pray for peace and good fortune, while boats burn in the water.

Taiwan is an **ISLAND** in the South China Sea.

Highest point: **JADE** Mountain, at 12,966 feet

Located on the Hengchun Peninsula, **KENTING** is Taiwan's only tropical national park.

The **LANTERN** Festival is celebrated in Taiwan each year.

Official language: **MANDARIN CHINESE**

The **MONKEY** Celebration marks the passage into manhood for the young boys of the Puyuma tribe.

Currency: **NEW TAIWAN DOLLAR**

PAISHA Island has an underwater tunnel where you can look into the sea.

Located in Taipei, the world's largest collection of Chinese art is held at the National **PALACE** Museum.

PEARL Milk Tea is a popular beverage snack here.

National flower: **PLUM** Blossom

Official name: **REPUBLIC** of China

With 101 stories, the Taipei 101 **SKYSCRAPER** is one of the top 10 tallest buildings in the world.

At 2,454 feet above sea level, **SUN MOON LAKE** is Taiwan's largest and deepest lake.

Capital: **TAIPEI**

In **TAROKO** National Park, there are natural marble caves.

The **TROPIC OF CANCER** crosses through Taiwan.

XIAOLIUQIU Island is one of the world's largest coral islands.

ZONGZI is a gooey rice dumpling wrapped in a leaf. It is traditionally eaten during the Dragon Boat Festival.

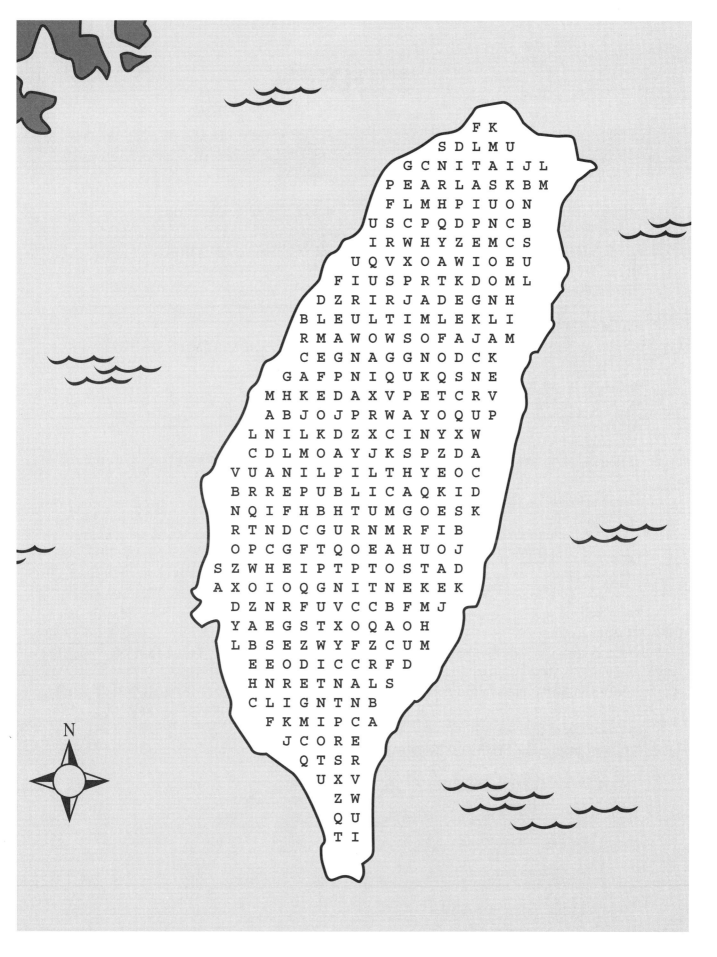

TURKEY

Capital: **ANKARA**

A cave in **ANTIOCH** is the location of the Church of St. Peter, the world's first cathedral.

ASIA MINOR, known as Anatolia, was once part of the Greco-Roman Empire. Turkey now occupies this land.

BACKGAMMON is a popular dice game played in Turkey.

BAKLAVA is a popular layered dessert made of pastry, honey, and chopped nuts.

The **BOSPORUS** strait connects the Sea of Marmara to the Black Sea.

The **DARDANELLES** strait connects the Sea of Marmara to the Aegean Sea.

Turkey lies in **EUROPE** *and which other continent?*

The Gediz Delta is a breeding ground for **FLAMINGOS**.

The world's first **ISLAMIC** University is located in Sanliurfa.

ISTANBUL is the world's only city located on two continents, Asia and Europe.

IZMIR is home to the temple of Artemis, one of the Seven Wonders of the Ancient World.

KADAYIF is a wheat pastry.

Currency: Turkish **LIRA**

Highest point: **MOUNT ARARAT**, at 16,946 feet

Turkey is famous for its **ORIENTAL RUGS**.

In 1513, Turkish cartographer **PIRI REIS** drew one of the first accurate world maps.

Government: **REPUBLIC** (headed by a prime minister)

Patara is the birthplace of St. Nicholas, who legend came to know as **SANTA CLAUS.**

A **SHISH KEBAB** is lamb, tomatoes, peppers, and onions skewered on a stick.

Official language: **TURKISH**

Official name: **TURKIYE CUMHURIYETI**, meaning "Republic of Turkey."

(Continent other than Europe in which Turkey lies: **Asia**)

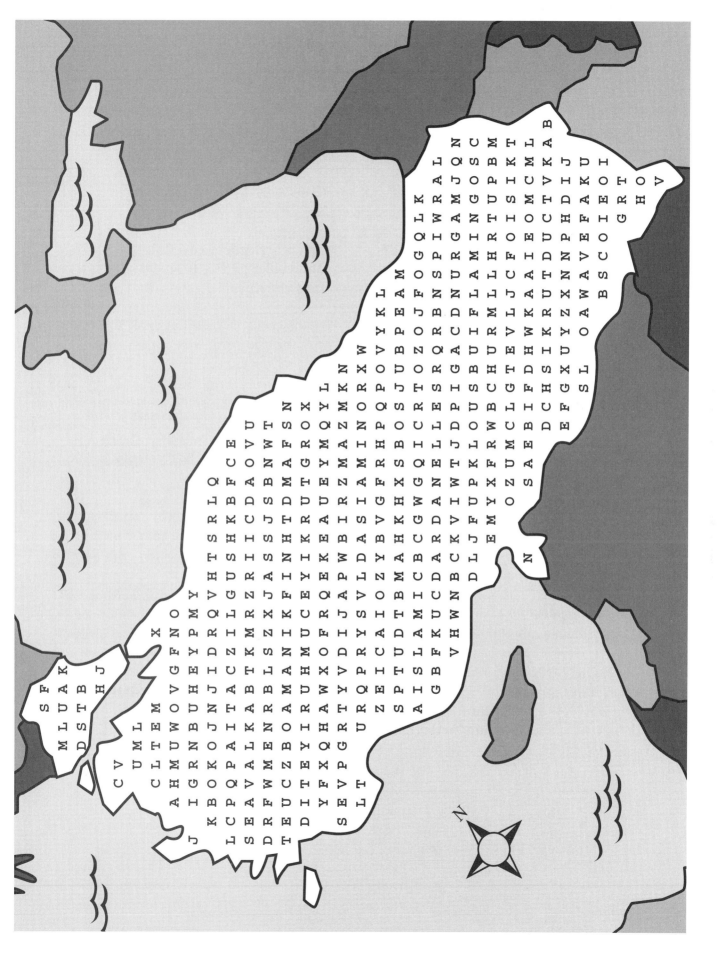

VIETNAM

An **AO DAI** is a long gown with loose-fitting pants, worn by a woman.

BICYCLES are a common mode of transportation.

CHO NOI is a floating market in the Mekong River Delta where people gather to exchange and sell supplies.

Government: **COMMUNIST** State (headed by a prime minister)

A **CYCLO** Taxi is a three-wheeled bicycle with a seat in the front for passengers.

DA NANG is one of Vietnam's largest cities.

Currency: Vietnamese **DONG**

Highest point: **FAN SI PAN**, at 10,312 feet

GREEN TEA is the most popular drink.

The **HA LONG** Bay is known for its islands, caves, and limestone rock pillars.

Capital: **HANOI**

The **HMONG** are an ethnic group of people who live in mountain villages.

HO CHI MINH CITY is Vietnam's largest city.

Bamboo **JACKS**, or Choi chuyen, is a popular game for girls.

KITES are made with flutes to make sounds like birds, car horns, and music when they fly.

During the **KY YEN** Festival, Vietnamese pray for good weather.

A **NON LA** is a pointed hat most people wear, to protect their faces from the sun.

Built in 1744, the Buddhist Giac Lam **PAGODA** is Ho Chi Minh City's oldest Buddhist temple.

The **POMELO** fruit grows in north, south, and central Vietnam, but it has a different taste and smell in each region.

Pho, a hot, sweet-smelling bowl of **RICE** noodle soup garnished with meat and other ingredients, is a typical dish here.

Spinning **TOPS** in streets and alleyways is a favorite activity for young children.

Official language: **VIETNAMESE**

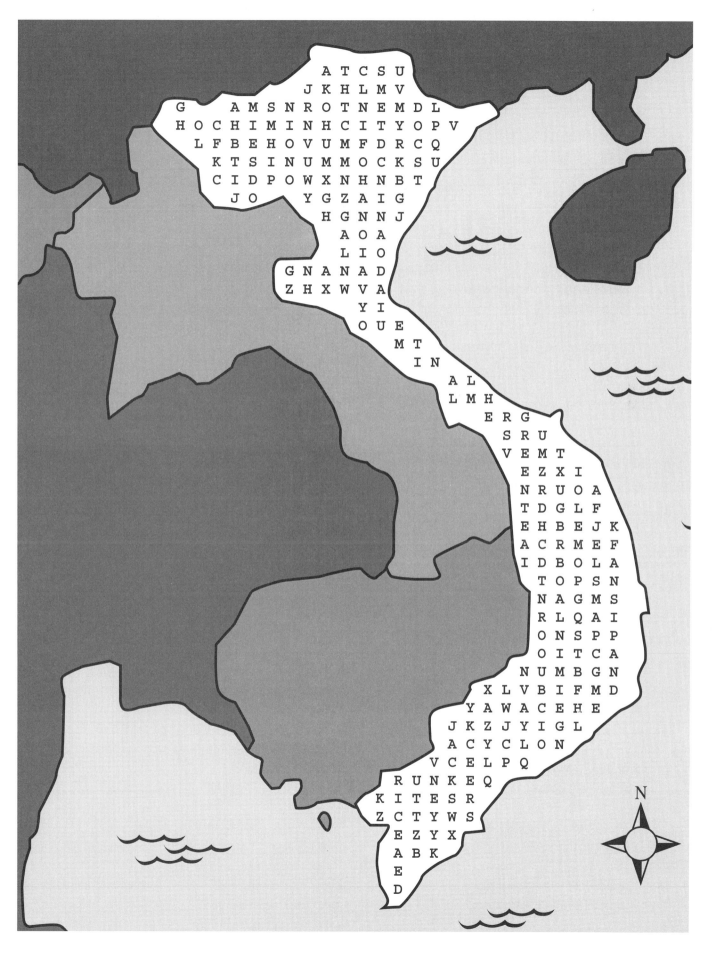

AUSTRALIA

The Tasmanian **BLUE GUM** is Tasmania's floral emblem.

Capital: **CANBERRA**

Official name: **COMMONWEALTH** of Australia

Australia is the only continent that is also a **COUNTRY**.

The capital of the Northern Territory is **DARWIN**.

Currency: Australian **DOLLAR**

Australia is called "The Land **DOWN UNDER**" because it is located in the Southern Hemisphere.

Australia has the second **DRIEST** climate on Earth. *Which continent has the driest climate?*

Official language: **ENGLISH**

The **GANG-GANG COCKATOO** is the Australian Capital Territory's animal emblem.

The **GREAT BARRIER REEF** is the world's largest coral reef.

The **HAIRY-NOSED WOMBAT** is South Australia's animal emblem.

The **KOALA** is **QUEENSLAND**'s animal emblem.

Lowest point: **LAKE EYRE**, at 52 feet below sea level

Government: Constitutional **MONARCHY** (headed by a prime minister)

Highest point: **MOUNT KOSCIUSZKO**, at 7,310 feet

The **NUMBAT** is Western Australia's animal emblem.

The **PLATYPUS** is New South Wales' animal emblem.

Leadbeater's **POSSUM** is Victoria's animal emblem.

The **ROYAL BLUEBELL** is the Australian Capital Territory's floral emblem.

At 2,970,000 square miles, Australia is the world's **SMALLEST** continent in area.

The capital of New South Wales is **SYDNEY**.

TASMANIA, an island off the southern coast of mainland Australia, is said to have the world's cleanest air and purest water.

WESTERN Australia is the largest state in Australia.

(Place with the driest climate on Earth: **Antarctica**)

48

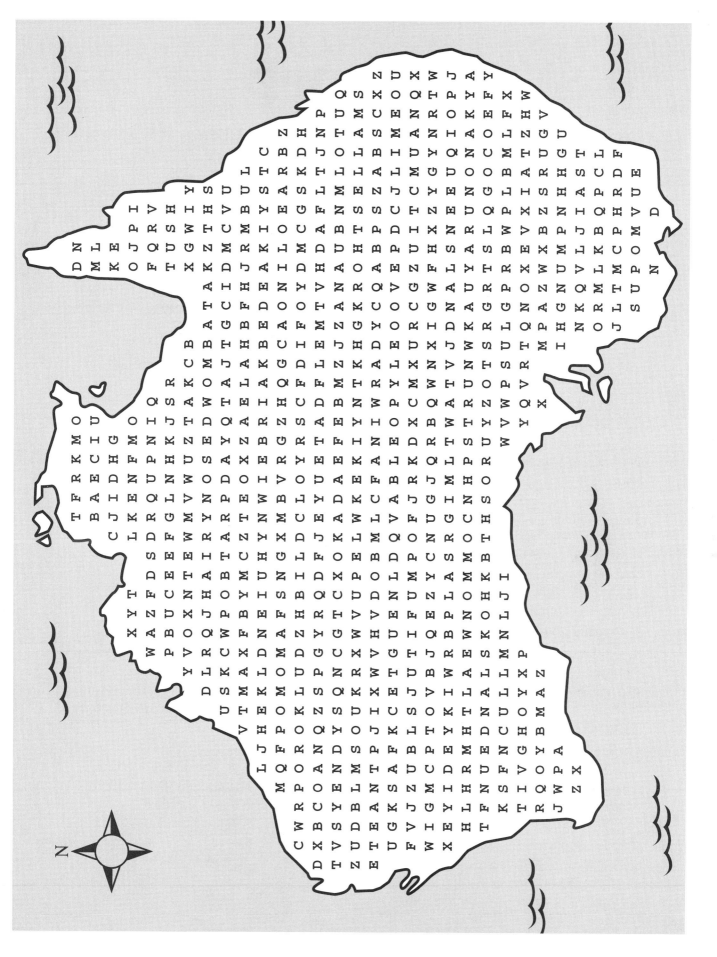

EUROPE

The **ALPS** are Europe's longest mountain chain, stretching about 750 miles long.

Europe has approximately 50 independent countries, including **AUSTRIA**, **BELARUS**, **HUNGARY**, **IRELAND**, **ITALY**, **SPAIN**, **SWITZERLAND**, and western **TURKEY**.

BOSNIA-HERZEGOVINA is home to Medjugorje, a special place for healing and spirituality.

The **CASPIAN SEA** is the world's largest enclosed body of water.

The **COLOSSUS OF RHODES** was one of the Seven Wonders of the Ancient World. It was located on an island in the Aegean Sea.

Bosnia-Herzegovina, **CROATIA**, **MACEDONIA**, **MONTENEGRO**, **SERBIA**, and **SLOVENIA** were once part of Yugoslavia.

In 1993, Czechoslovakia split into the **CZECH REPUBLIC** and **SLOVAKIA**.

Scandinavia is made up of **DENMARK**, **NORWAY**, and **SWEDEN**.

ESTONIA, **LATVIA**, and **LITHUANIA** are the Baltic States.

The English Channel separates **FRANCE** *from which other European country?*

The Statue of Zeus located in **GREECE** was one of the Seven Wonders of the Ancient World.

ICELAND is an island country below the Arctic Circle.

MONACO is the world's second smallest country.

Highest point: **MOUNT ELBRUS**, at 18,510 feet

The Eiffel Tower is located in **PARIS**, the capital of France.

POLAND became an independent republic in 1918.

The capital of **PORTUGAL** is Lisbon.

RUSSIA is the world's largest country.

SAN MARINO is the world's oldest republic.

At approximately 4 million square miles, Europe is the world's **SIXTH** largest continent in area.

The **UNITED KINGDOM** consists of England, Scotland, Wales, and Northern Ireland.

VATICAN CITY is the world's smallest country.

At 2,293 miles, the **VOLGA** River is Europe's longest river. *Do you know in which country it is located?*

(Country in which the Volga River is located: **Russia**)

(Country separated from France by the English Channel: **Great Britain**)

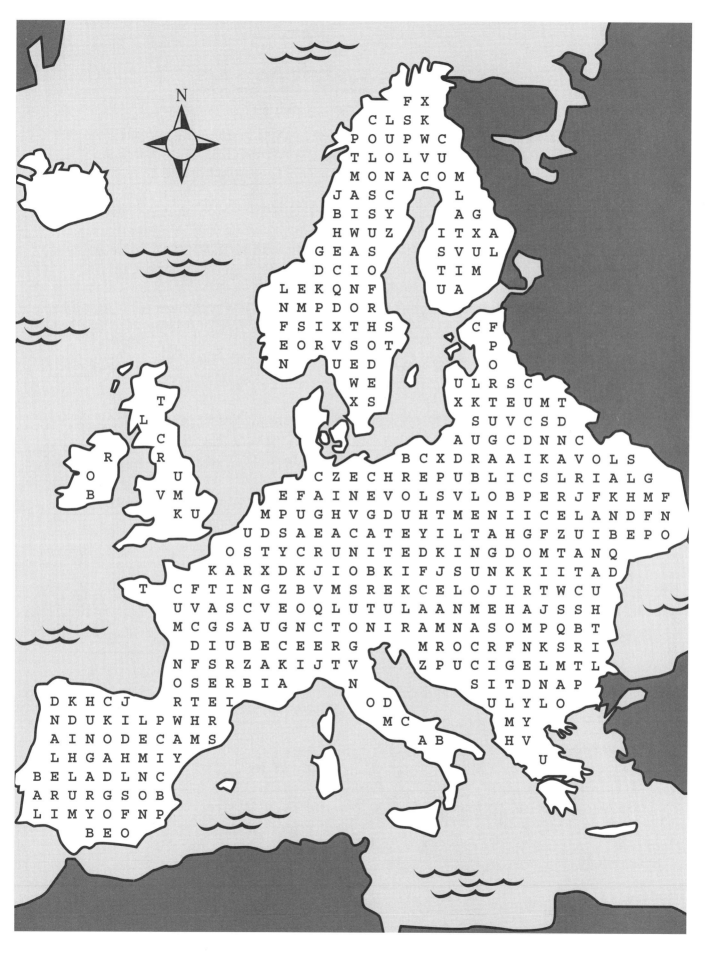

CZECH REPUBLIC

The **BOHEMIAN** Forest is located in the southwestern part of the country.

Built in 1357, the Charles **BRIDGE** is one of the Czech Republic's oldest bridges.

BRNO is the Czech Republic's second largest city.

The president lives in the Prague **CASTLE**.

Official name: **CESKA REPUBLIKA**, meaning "Czech Republic."

Founded in 1348, **CHARLES** University is one of Europe's oldest universities.

Alois Wessel created Czech's curd **CHEESE** in 1876.

A **COMPUTER** was invented here that is operated by the eye.

Official language: **CZECH**

Lowest point: **ELBE RIVER**, at 377 feet

The Elbe River Valley in Bohemia provides **FARMERS** with fertile ground for crops such as rye and wheat.

KARLOVY VARY is a famous health resort known for its mineral springs.

Currency: Czech **KORUNA**

Acid rain and pollution threaten wildlife in the **KRKONOSE** Mountains, located in the northern part of the country.

LACROSSE is a popular sport here.

Czechs and **MORAVIANS** make up most of the Czech Republic's population.

The **MUNICH** Agreement was signed in 1938, giving the Sudetenland to Germany.

The **NATIONAL** Theater in Prague is one of the Czech Republic's oldest theaters.

Government: **PARLIAMENTARY DEMOCRACY** (headed by a Prime Minister)

PLZEN is home to Europe's second-largest synagogue.

Capital: **PRAGUE**

Highest point: **SNEZKA**, at 5,256 feet

Apple **STRUDEL** is a favorite dessert.

SUDETENLAND became part of the Czech Republic in 1993. It is a forested and mountainous region.

Communist control ended with the **VELVET REVOLUTION**.

The **VLTAVA** River runs through the city of Prague.

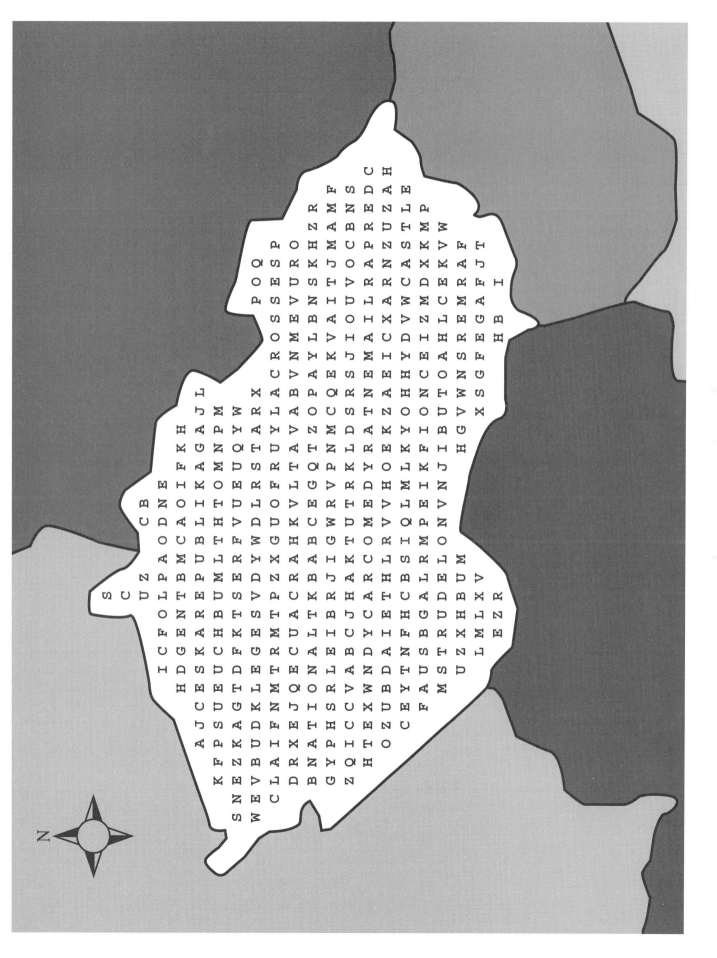

FRANCE

AMIENS was the headquarters for Julius Caesar during the Gallic War in 54 BCE.

The **BRIARD**, a dog about 25 inches tall, with long, wavy hair, was first bred in France.

BURGUNDY is France's leading grape growing region.

CANNES is home to the annual Cannes Film Festival, one of the world's oldest and most prestigious film festivals.

CORSICA is an island located in the Mediterranean Sea.

The **EIFFEL TOWER**, located in Paris, is 1,063 feet tall with its antenna.

Currency: **EURO**. *What was the original currency of France called?*

Paris is known as "The **FASHION** Capital of the World."

Official language: **FRENCH**

LE MANS is home to a 24-hour motorbike race.

The **LOIRE RIVER** is France's longest river.

Located in Paris, the **LOUVRE** is one of the world's largest art museums.

The Rhône and the Saône rivers divide the city of **LYON** into three parts.

The **MARSEILLAISE** is France's national anthem.

MERCI means "thank you" in French.

Highest point: **MONT BLANC**, at 15,771 feet

Joan of Arc led French troops during the fight against England over **NORMANDY**.

King Louis XIV built the **PALACE OF VERSAILLES** in the 1600s. It has 700 rooms.

From 1309 until 1377, the popes lived in the **PAPAL PALACE**, located in Avignon.

Capital: **PARIS**

Government: **REPUBLIC** (headed by a prime minister)

Official name: **REPUBLIQUE FRANÇAISE**, meaning "French Republic."

SALUT means "hello" in French.

Paris is the birthplace of sculptor Auguste Rodin. One of his most famous sculptures is "**THE THINKER**."

The first **TOUR DE FRANCE** bicycle race took place in 1903.

(Original currency of France: **French franc.**)

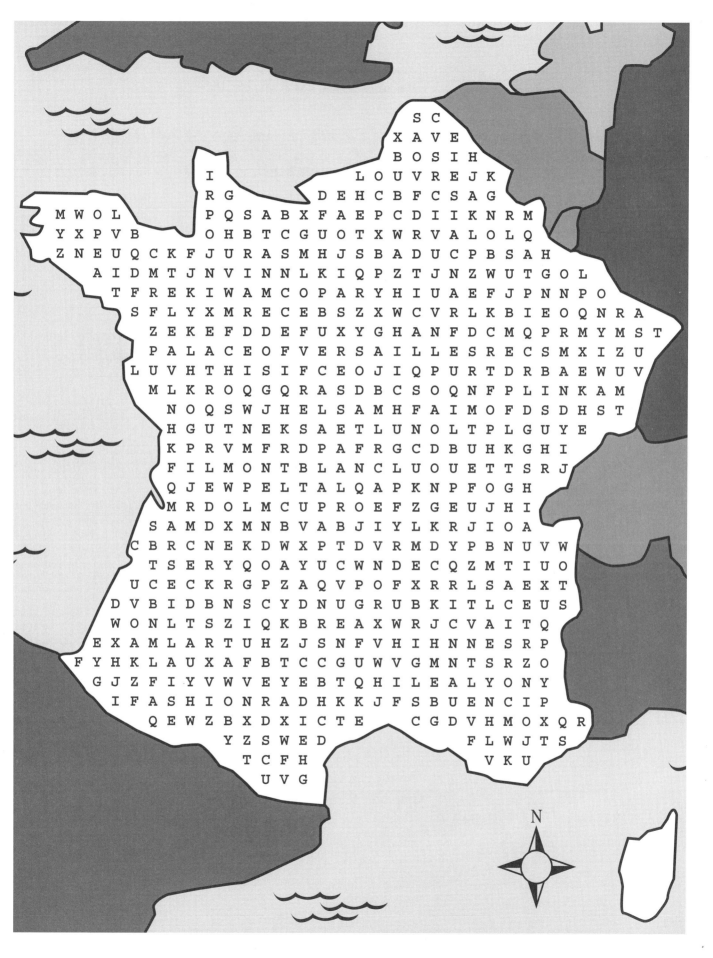

GERMANY

Germany's multiple-lane highways are called **AUTOBAHNS**.

Germany's highest point is located in the **BAVARIAN ALPS**.

Germany is the birthplace of composer Ludwig van **BEETHOVEN**.

Capital: **BERLIN**

The **BERLIN WALL** was taken down in 1989, uniting East and West Berlin under Germany's non-communist government.

Toys, radios, and musical instruments are made in the **BLACK FOREST**.

BONN was the capital of West Germany. After East Germany and West Germany reunified in 1990, Berlin became the capital in 1999.

Official name: **BUNDESREPUBLIK DEUTSCHLAND**, meaning "Federal Republic of Germany."

The city of **DRESDEN** is a major art center in Europe.

Currency: **EURO**. *What was the original currency of Germany called?*

Government: **FEDERAL REPUBLIC** (headed by a federal chancellor)

In the 1990s, a team at the **FRAUNHOFER INSTITUTE** invented the MP3.

Official language: **GERMAN**

HAMBURG is Germany's second largest city.

The first world's fair held in Germany took place in **HANOVER** in 2000.

The University of **HEIDELBERG** is Germany's oldest university.

MUNICH is Germany's third largest city and home to the BMW automobile headquarters.

OKTOBERFEST is a festival held each autumn in Munich.

SAARLAND is home to coal mines and steel plants.

SAUERKRAUT was invented while trying to keep cabbage from spoiling.

A stage performance known as **SINGSPIEL**, that mixes music and spoken dialogue, originated here.

The Peace of Westphalia treaty ended the **THIRTY YEARS' WAR**. *What year was it signed? What **TREATY** ended World War I?*

Highest point: **ZUGSPITZE**, at 9,721 feet

(Original currency of Germany: **Deutsche Mark**)

(Year in which the Peace of Westphalia was signed: **1648**; Treaty that ended World War I: **Treaty of Versailles**)

IRELAND

The island of Ireland is divided into two parts. **NORTHERN** Ireland is part of the United Kingdom. The Southern part of Ireland is officially known as the **REPUBLIC** of **IRELAND**.

To kiss the **BLARNEY** stone you must lean backwards over a railing. It is located in the Blarney Castle and Rock Close in Cork.

Highest point: **CARRAUNTOOHIL**, at 3,414 feet

CORK is Ireland's largest county.

Capital of the Republic of Ireland: **DUBLIN**

The **EAGLE** Wing Festival celebrates cultural relations between Ireland and America.

Official languages: **ENGLISH** and **IRISH**

Currency of the Republic of Ireland: **EURO**. *What was the original currency of Ireland called?*

Located in Dublin, **GRAFTON STREET** is lined with shopping areas, tearooms, and more.

Official Emblem of the Republic of Ireland: **HARP**

HORSE RACING is a popular sport here.

*The **IRISH SEA** and **SAINT GEORGE'S** Channel separate Ireland from which country?*

IRISH STEW is a traditional dish that contains potatoes, onions, and mutton boiled in a pot.

The River **LIFFEY** runs through the capital of Northern Ireland, Dublin.

Lakes are called **LOUGHS** here.

LOUTH is Ireland's smallest county.

The **O'CONNELL BRIDGE** connects the two sections of Dublin.

Over 3,000 **PARADES** are held during Marching Season, which takes place from spring to early fall.

RUGBY, a sport similar to football, is popular here.

Ireland's longest river is the River **SHANNON**.

Ireland is sometimes called "**THE EMERALD ISLE**," because of all the greenery.

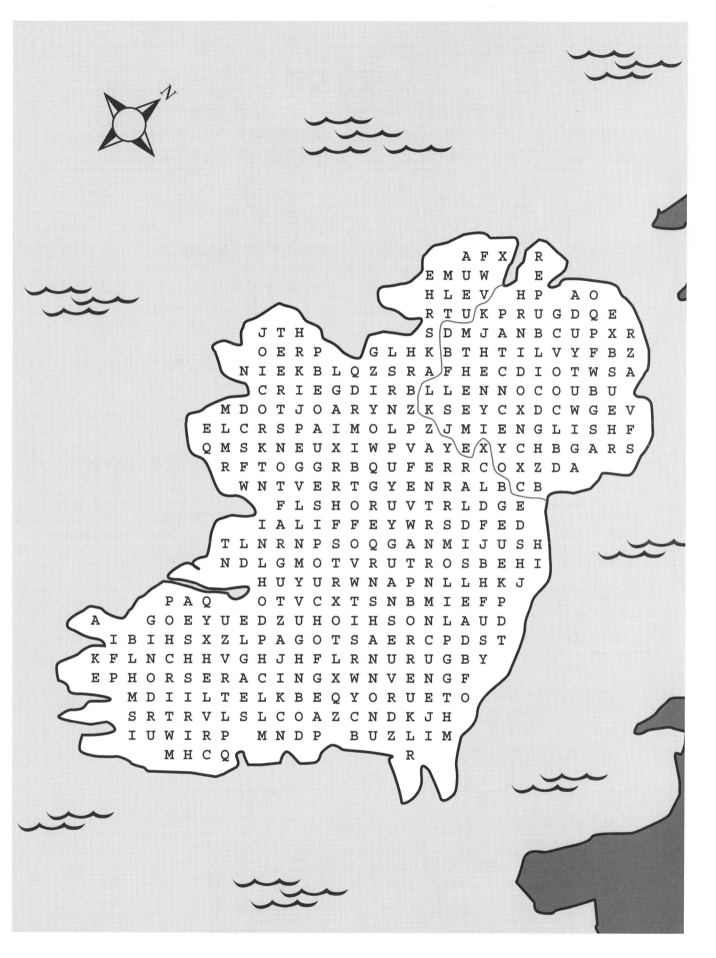

ITALY

Mount **ETNA** is an active volcano located on the island of Sicily.

Currency: **EURO**. *What was the original currency called?*

The three colors on the Italian **FLAG** are green (hope), white (faith), and red (charity).

Lake **GARDA** is Italy's largest lake.

Official language: **ITALIAN**

The **LEANING TOWER** of Pisa leans 12 feet, 10 inches out of line.

A **LEGHORN** is a straw hat made in Tuscany.

The Strait of **MESSINA** in the Mediterranean Sea separates Sicily from Italy's mainland.

MILAN is Italy's second largest city.

Highest point: **MONT BLANC** (or, in Italian, Monte Blanco), at 15,771

Government: **PARLIAMENTARY** Democracy (headed by a prime minister)

PARMESAN cheese has become a symbol of the city of Parma.

A **PASSEGGIATA** is a family stroll many enjoy on a Sunday.

National dish: **PASTA**

The **PITTI** Palace is Italy's largest palace.

Raffaele Esposito invented **PIZZA** in 1889.

Official name: **REPUBBLICA** Italiana, meaning "Italian Republic."

Capital: **ROME**

SARDINIA and **SICILY** are Italy's two largest islands.

The **SEVEN HILLS** of Rome, on which the country was built, include Aventine, Caelian, Capitoline, Esquiline, Palatine, Quirinal, and Viminal.

VENICE is made up of 118 islands, so people must use boats to get from one place to another.

(Original Italian currency: **Italian lira**)

POLAND

The **BELOVEZHSKAYA** Forest is known as "The King of the Forest."

BUREK is Poland's most popular name for a dog.

CAMPING is a favorite activity here.

Poland has one of the world's richest **COAL FIELDS**.

Deepest lake: **HANCZA**, at 354 feet deep

Founded in 1364, the **JAGIELLONIAN** University was Poland's first Polish university.

Poland has over 9,300 **LAKES**.

LÓDŹ is Poland's second largest city.

The Polish **LOWLAND SHEEPDOG** was bred here to herd sheep.

Lake **MAMRY** and Lake **SNIARDWY** are Poland's largest lakes.

Official language: **POLISH**

National dance: **POLONAISE**

Many people use the **RAILROAD** as a means of transportation.

Government: **REPUBLIC** (headed by a prime minister)

Highest point: **RYSY PEAK**, at 8,199 feet

Official name: **RZECZYPOSPOLITA POLSKA**, meaning "Republic of Poland."

The **SWIETOKRZYSKIE** Mountains are Poland's oldest mountain range.

The **VISTULA** is Poland's longest river.

Capital: **WARSAW**

National symbol: **WHITE-TAILED EAGLE**

Located in Krakow, the underground **WIELICZKA** salt mine contains an entire town. Stairs and chandeliers there are made of salt.

WOLINSKI National Park is Poland's first maritime national park.

Currency: Polish **ZLOTY**

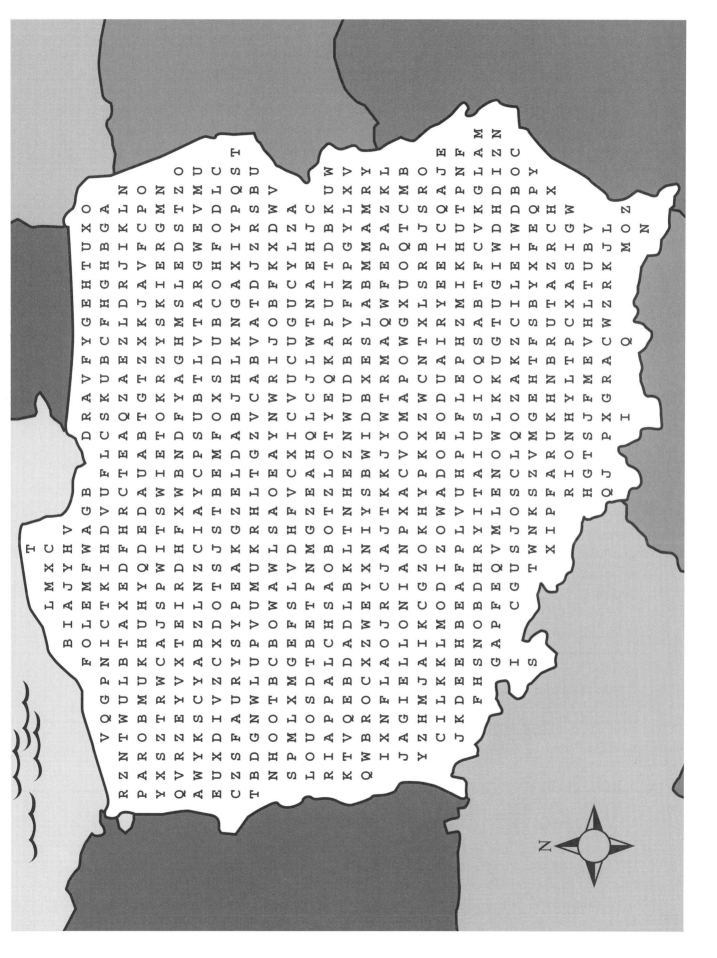

ROMANIA

BEARS' CAVE got its name from mine workers who found 15,000-year-old bear skeletons in 1975.

Capital: **BUCHAREST**

Lake **BUCURA** is Romania's largest lake.

The **DANUBE** River is Romania's longest river.

The Danube-Black Sea Canal that flows through **DOBRUJA** is a shortcut from the Danube River to the Black Sea.

Located in Transylvania, the Bran Castle was the inspiration for the novel **DRACULA**.

There are about 2,500 **LAKES** in Romania.

The **MAIDENS' FAIR** is held each July when all go to the Gaina Mountain in hopes of finding someone to love.

MAMALIGA is a porridge made from corn meal.

A **MITITEI** is a grilled skinless sausage.

Highest point: **MOUNT MOLDOVEANU**, at 8,343 feet

A **PAPANASI** is a cottage cheese donut with sour cream.

The **PIETROSU PEAK**, located in Calimani National Park, is the highest massif in Romania's volcanic chain.

Government: **REPUBLIC** (headed by a prime minister)

Official name: **REPUBLICA ROMANIA**, meaning "Republic of Romania."

Established in 1935, **RETEZAT** National Park is Romania's oldest national park.

Official language: **ROMANIAN**

Currency: **ROMANIAN LEU**

Located in Brasov, **ROPE STREET** is one of Europe's narrowest streets, at four feet wide.

A **SARMALE** is a cabbage leaf stuffed with meat, rice, and spices.

TRANSYLVANIA is Romania's largest region.

WALACHIA is Romania's most populated area.

Lake **ZANOAGA** is Romania's deepest lake.

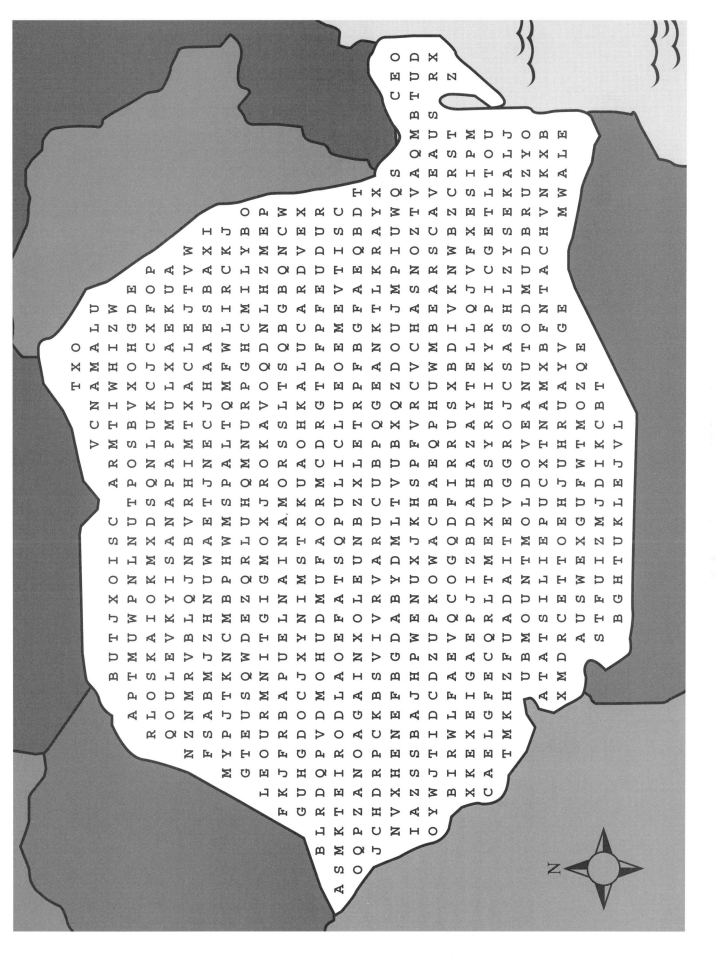

RUSSIA

Russia stretches into **ASIA** and **EUROPE**.

At 5,315 feet deep, Lake **BAIKAL** is the world's deepest lake.

BALLET plays an important part in Russian culture.

The **CASPIAN SEA** is a saltwater lake and the world's largest inland body of water.

The Palace of the **FACETS** is Moscow's smallest palace.

At 15,584 feet, **KLYUCHEVSKAYA** Volcano is Russia's tallest volcano.

The Moscow **KREMLIN** complex is home to palaces, the Red Square, and the president's home.

At 6,835 square miles, Lake **LADOGA** is Europe's largest lake.

At 6,592,812 square miles, Russia is the world's **LARGEST COUNTRY**. *What is the world's second largest country?*

The **LENINGRADSKY** Rail Terminal is Russia's oldest train station.

Capital: **MOSCOW**

Highest point: **MOUNT ELBRUS**, at 18,510 feet. This is Europe's highest point.

PERMAFROST is permanently frozen soil located in the tundra region in the north.

In 1958, the **POKLONNAJA** Mountain was established in honor of those who lost their lives during the Great Patriot War.

Located in Moscow, **RED SQUARE** is a main gathering place.

Government: **REPUBLIC** (headed by a prime minister)

Official names: **ROSSIYA**, meaning "Russia," or Rossiyskaya Federatsiya, meaning "Russian Federation."

Currency: Russian **RUBLE**

Official language: **RUSSIAN**

The endangered Amur **TIGER** can be found in southeastern Russia.

The **URAL MOUNTAINS** separate the European and Asian sides of Russia.

Russia gained its independence in 1991 when the **USSR** officially disbanded.

The **VOLGA RIVER** is European Russia's longest river.

(World's second largest country: **Canada**)

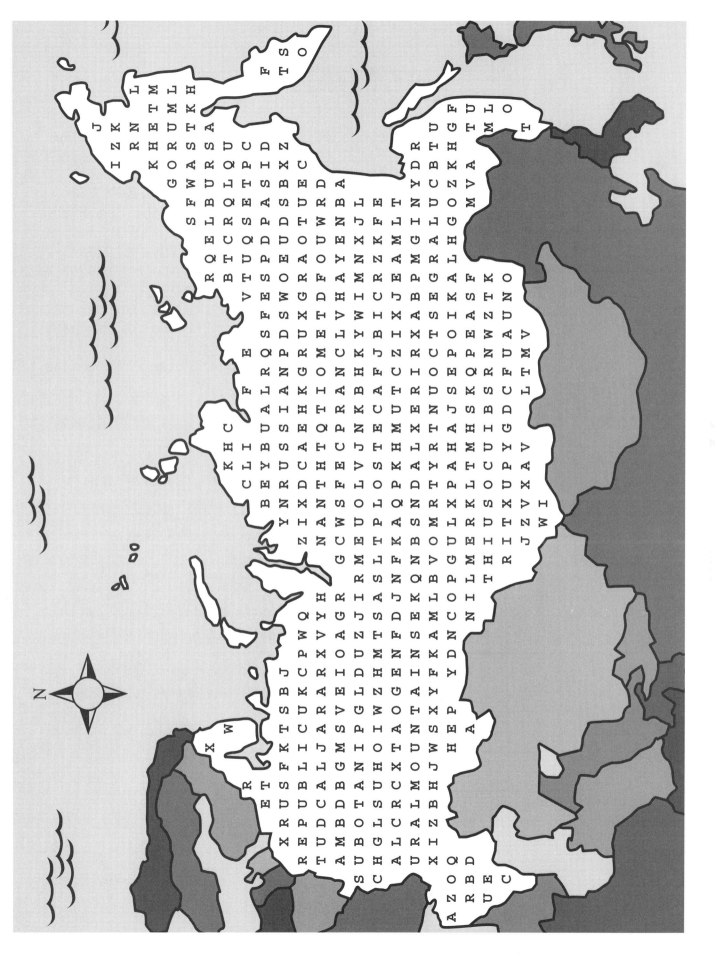

SLOVAKIA

The Great **BUSTARD** (*Otis tarda*) is Europe's biggest bird.

Lowest point: **BODROG** River, at 312 feet

Capital: **BRATISLAVA**

Slovenska **BRYNDZA** is sheep cheese that is only produced in Slovakia.

The Krasnohorska Jaskyna **CAVE** is home to the world's tallest stalagmite.

The Tatranska Madonna is the world's largest mosaic made from circulating **COINS**.

In 1993, **CZECHOSLOVAKIA** split into two countries, Slovakia and the Czech Republic.

Government: Parliamentary **DEMOCRACY** (headed by a prime minister)

Currency: **EURO**. *What was the original currency of Slovakia called?*

Highest point: **GERLACHOVSKY** stit, at 8,711 feet

GOULASH is a popular stew, flavored with paprika.

ICE HOCKEY is the most popular sport here.

Located in the high tatras, **KMET'OV** Vodopád is Slovakia's highest waterfall.

The **KREMNICA MINT** is one of the world's oldest coin producers, and makes the Slovak Euro coin.

NITRA is one of Slovakia's oldest towns.

Stefan Banic from Slovakia invented the **PARACHUTE** in 1913.

Official name: Slovenska **REPUBLIKA**, meaning "Slovak Republic."

The **SEA EAGLE** is Slovakia's biggest bird.

SKIING is a popular sport here.

Official language: **SLOVAK**

The **TATRA CHAMOIS** is similar to a goat and can only be found in the Tatra Mountains.

VRBOVÉ is home to the leaning Bell Tower.

(Original currency of Slovakia: **Slovak Koruna**)

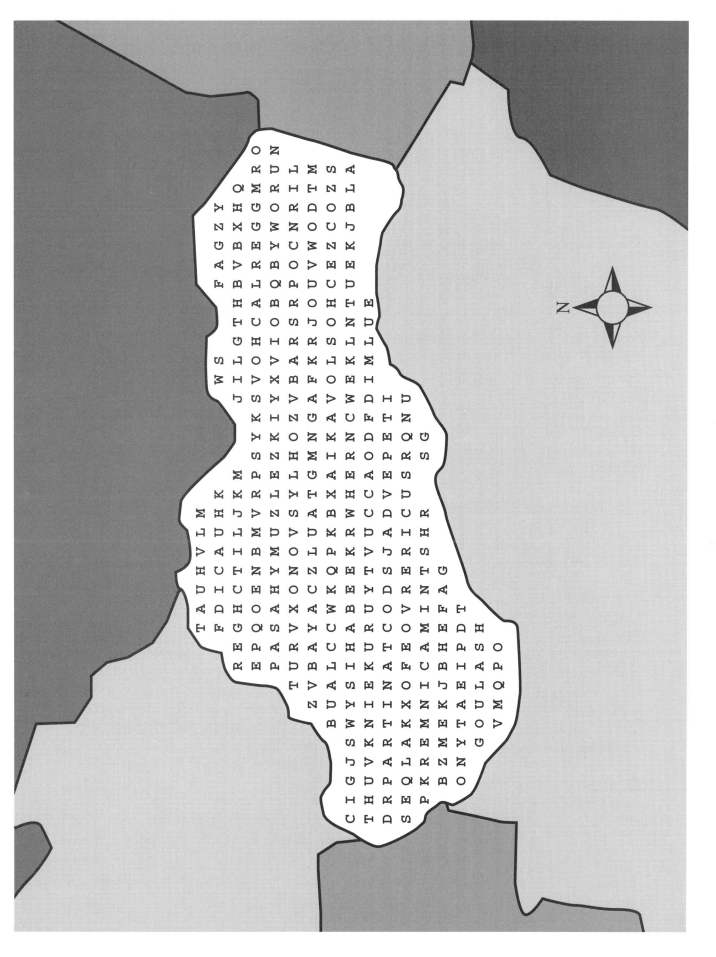

SPAIN

The **BALEARIC** Islands are part of Spain and are located in the Mediterranean Sea.

BARCELONA is Spain's second largest city.

Spain is known for **BULLFIGHTING**.

One of Europe's oldest cities is believed to be **CÁDIZ**.

Spain's two provinces that make up the **CANARY** Islands in the Atlantic Ocean are Santa Cruz de Tenerife and Las Palmas.

Located in Barcelona, the **CASA MILA** is a unique building designed by architect Antonió Gaudí.

Official language: **CASTILIAN SPANISH**

CHURROS are strips of fried dough, and are usually served with hot chocolate.

The **EBRO RIVER** is one of Spain's longest rivers.

Currency: **EURO**. *What was the original currency of Spain called?*

EUSKARA is Europe's oldest language still in use, and is only spoken by northern people called **BASQUES**.

FLAMENCO is a popular Spanish folk dance form.

The **GUADALQUIVIR BASIN** lies in the hottest part of Spain.

The **IBERIAN** *Peninsula is made up of Spain and what other country?*

JOYO is bread covered with olive oil that is given out during the Olive Festival.

Capital: **MADRID**

PAELLA is a popular dish that is made of rice mixed with seafood and vegetables.

Government: **PARLIAMENTARY MONARCHY** (headed by a prime minister)

A **PASEO** is a walk many people take after the evening meal.

Pablo **PICASSO** (1881–1973) is one of Spain's most famous painters.

Highest point: **PICO DE TEIDE**, at 12,198 feet

The **PYRENEES** *Mountains separate Spain from what other country?*

In July, the city of Pamplona hosts the famous **RUNNING OF THE BULLS**.

The **TAGUS** is Spain's longest river.

(Country separated from Spain by the Pyrenees: **France**)

(Country other than Spain that makes up the Iberian Peninsula: **Portugal**)

(Original currency of Spain: **Peseta**)

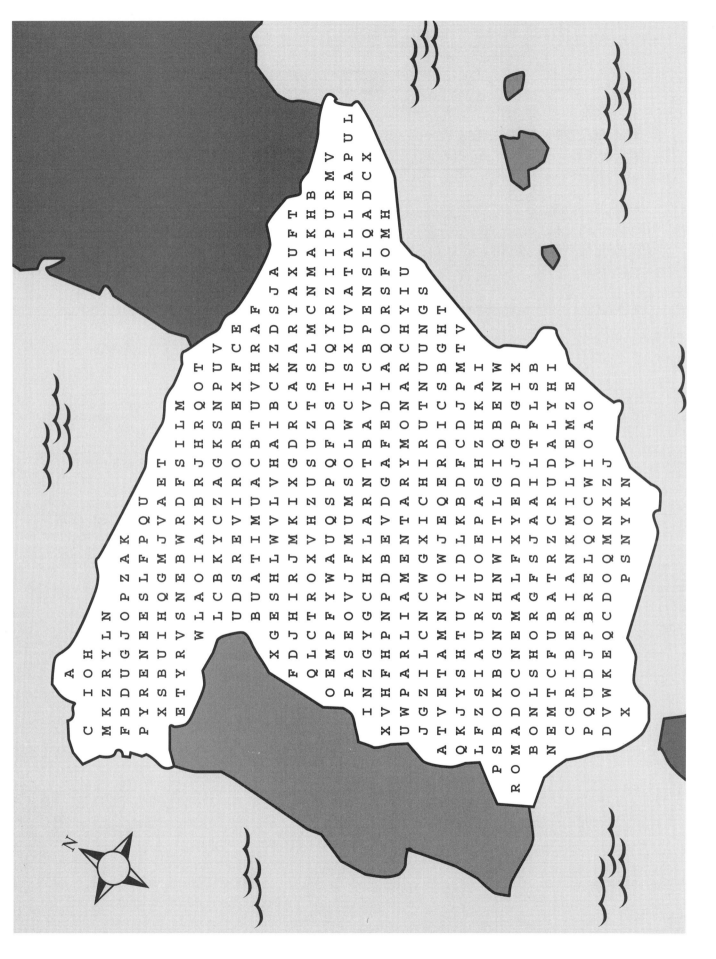

SWEDEN

The **AURORA BOREALIS** can be viewed above the Arctic Circle between September and March.

The government helps citizens with free **EDUCATION**, **HEALTH** insurance, annual pensions for those in need, and social security.

FINNISH people are Sweden's largest ethnic minority.

More than half of the country is covered in **FORESTS**.

GOTLAND and **ÖLAND** are two popular vacation islands located in the Baltic Sea.

GYMNASTICS are a popular form of exercise here.

Highest point: Mount **KEBNEKAISE**, at 6,926 feet

A **KING** or **QUEEN** is the head of state.

Official name: **KONUNGARIKET SVERIGE**, meaning "Kingdom of Sweden."

Currency: Swedish **KRONA**

At 2,156 square miles, **LAKE VANERN** is one of Europe's largest lakes.

The northernmost part of the country is known as the **LAPLAND**, or Sápmi.

Swedish native Astrid **LINDGREN** (1907–2002) is known for writing the Pippi Longstocking children's books.

Carolus **LINNAEUS** (1707–1778) is known for his system of naming plants and animals by group and kind.

Government: Constitutional **MONARCHY** (headed by a prime minister)

The **ORESUND LINK** connects Sweden and Denmark.

Sweden, Norway, and Denmark are the three **SCANDINAVIAN** countries.

A large self-serve table of hot and cold foods is known as a **SMORGASBORD**.

Capital: **STOCKHOLM**

Official language: **SWEDISH**

The **VASA RACE** is a ski race held each March in Dalarna.

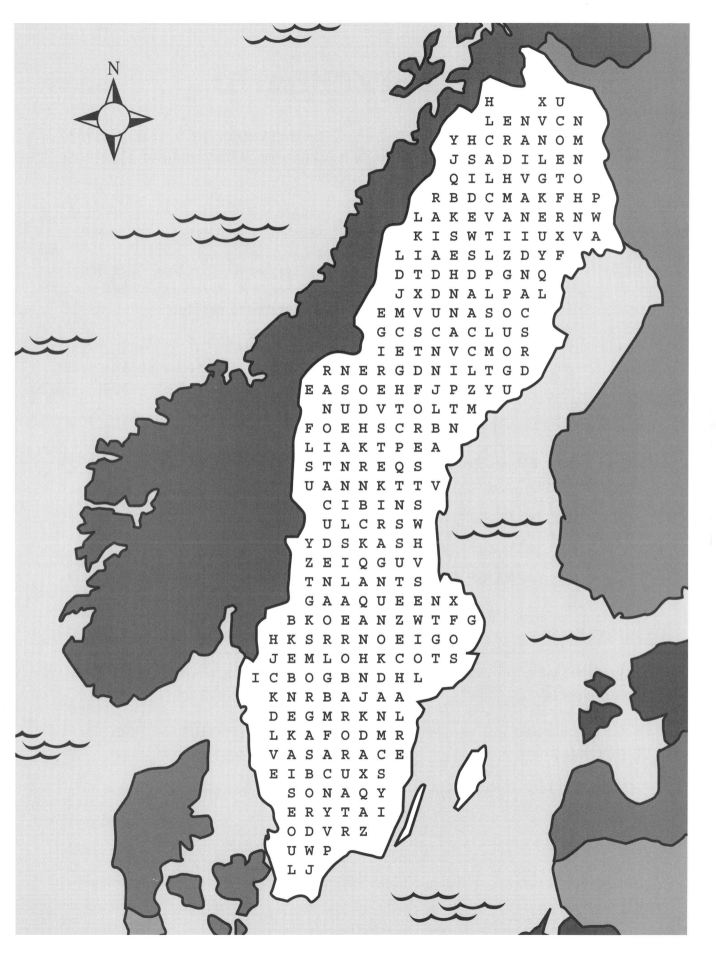

SWITZERLAND

Founded in 1460, the University of **BASEL** is Switzerland's oldest university.

Capital: **BERN**

Swiss states are called **CANTONS**.

CERN is the world's largest research center for **SUBATOMIC** particles.

Government: **CONFEDERATION** (The power is divided between central and state governments.)

At 5,100 feet above sea level, **DAVOS** is Switzerland's highest city.

Highest point: **DUFOURSPITZE** of Monte Rosa, at 15,203 feet

Albert **EINSTEIN** wrote his theory of relativity in Bern.

Currency: Swiss **FRANC**

Official languages: **FRENCH**, **GERMAN**, and **ITALIAN**

Lake **GENEVA** is one of central Europe's largest lakes.

HELVETIA is the Latin name for Switzerland.

HORNUSSEN is a popular sport similar to baseball.

*The **MATTERHORN** is located on the borders of Switzerland and what other country?*

Men are required to train at age 20 for the citizens' army known as the **MILITIA**.

The Greater Swiss **MOUNTAIN DOG** was bred in Switzerland and used to pull carts and herd livestock.

In **MUOTA VALLEY**, six people predict the weather by observing the behavior of animals, winds, ants, plants, and water sources.

Located in the Alps, **SAINT MORITZ** is a popular resort town.

Official name in German: **SCHWEIZ**

Official name in French: **SUISSE**

Official name in Italian: **SVIZZERA**

The **SWATCH GROUP** is the world's largest watchmaker.

TICINO hosts the annual spring Camellia Festival.

Universities are **TUITION FREE** for students.

ZURICH is Switzerland's largest city.

(Country other than Switzerland in which the Matterhorn is located: **Italy**)

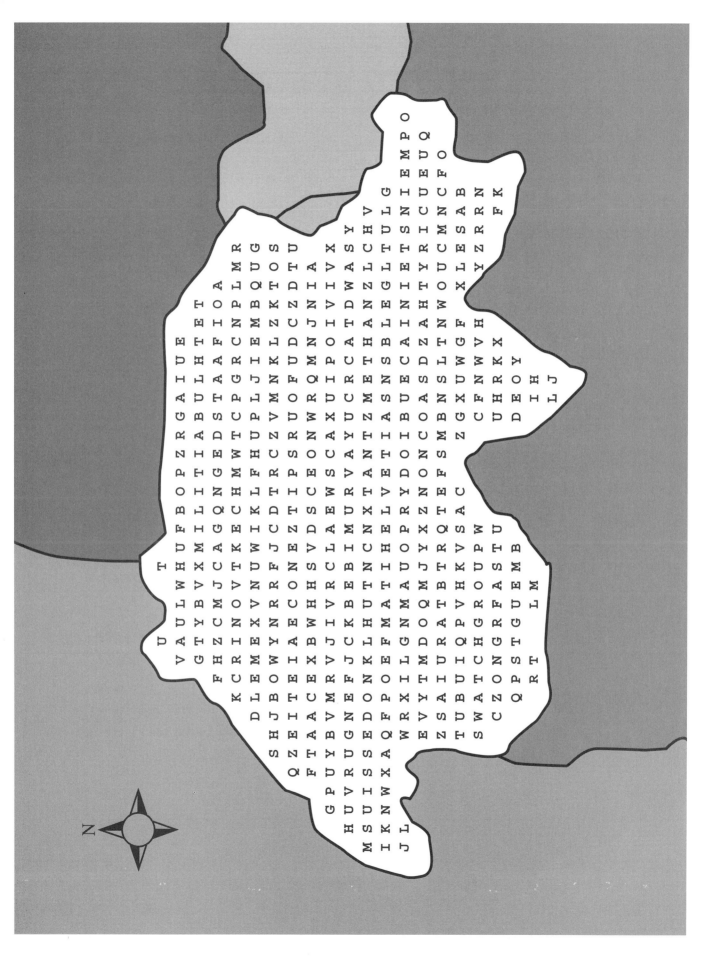

UNITED KINGDOM

Capital of Northern Ireland: **BELFAST**

Highest point in Scotland and the United Kingdom: **BEN NEVIS**, at 4,406 feet

BONNYBRIDGE is known as the world's number one spot to view UFOs.

Capital of Wales: **CARDIFF**

The English **CHANNEL** *separates the island of Great Britain from what other country?*

Government: Parliamentary **DEMOCRACY** (headed by a prime minister)

Capital of Scotland: **EDINBURGH**

ENGLAND, **SCOTLAND**, **WALES**, and **NORTHERN IRELAND** are the four nations that make up the United Kingdom.

Official language: **ENGLISH**

National anthem: "**GOD SAVE** the Queen"

GOLF was invented in Scotland.

GREAT BRITAIN is made up of England, Scotland, and Wales.

A **KING** or **QUEEN** is the head of state.

LAWN BOWLING is a popular sport here.

Capital of England and of the United Kingdom: **LONDON**

Currency: British **POUND**

Highest point in England: **SCAFELL PIKE**, at 3,210 feet

The **SEVERN** River and the **THAMES** River are the United Kingdom's longest rivers.

The Shetland pony and the Shetland Sheepdog were first bred on **SHETLAND** Islands off the coast of Scotland.

Highest point in Northern Ireland: **SLIEVE DONARD**, at 2,796 feet

Highest point in Wales: **SNOWDON**, at 3,561 feet

The railway **TUNNEL** *beneath the English Channel links the United Kingdom to which other country?*

Official name: **UNITED KINGDOM** of Great Britain and Northern Ireland

(Country separated from the United Kingdom by the English Channel: **France**)

(Country linked to the United Kingdom by a railway tunnel beneath the English Channel: **France**)

NORTH AMERICA

The world's smallest ocean, the **ARCTIC** Ocean, extends alongside North America's northern border.

The world's second largest ocean, the **ATLANTIC** Ocean, extends alongside North America's eastern border.

CANADA and the **UNITED STATES OF AMERICA** are sometimes called "Anglo-America," because of their British ancestors.

Belize, Costa Rica, El Salvador, Guatemala, Honduras, Nicaragua, and Panama make up **CENTRAL** America.

CUBA and **JAMAICA** are two of the island nations in the Caribbean Sea.

The West Indies' second largest island, Hispaniola, consists of the **DOMINICAN REPUBLIC** on the east and **HAITI** on the west.

Lake **ERIE**, Lake **HURON**, Lake **MICHIGAN**, Lake **ONTARIO**, and Lake **SUPERIOR** are North America's five Great Lakes. *Which one lies only in the United States?*

GREENLAND is the world's largest island.

Highest point: Mount **MCKINLEY**, at 20,320 feet. *Where is this mountain located?*

Mexico, Central America, and the Caribbean Islands are sometimes called "**MIDDLE** America," because they lie between the United States and South America.

The waters of Lake Erie and Lake Ontario meet to make the world-famous **NIAGARA FALLS** in the United States and Canada.

The world's largest body of water, the **PACIFIC** Ocean, stretches alongside North America's western border.

The **ROCKY** Mountains are North America's largest mountain chain. They run from Canada to New Mexico in the United States.

At 9,400,000 square miles, North America is the world's **THIRD** largest continent in area.

TRINIDAD AND TOBAGO are two islands but one country in the West Indies.

The **WEST INDIES** are a group of islands in the Caribbean Sea.

(Where Mt. McKinley is located: **Alaska**)

(The only Great Lake to lie entirely in the United States: **Lake Michigan**)

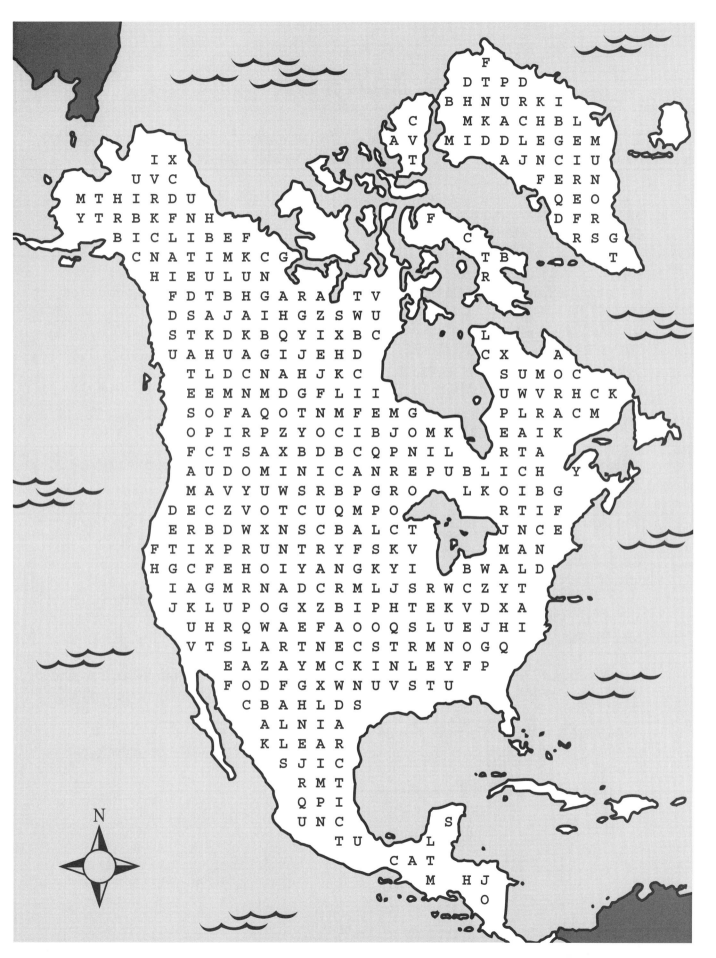

CANADA

The **AURORA BOREALIS** can be seen here all year.

The **CALGARY STAMPEDE** is a famous annual event featuring a rodeo and other Old West activities.

CANADA DAY is celebrated each July 1 in honor the Dominion of Canada.

Drumheller Valley is known as the "**DINOSAUR** Capital of the World," because remains of many dinosaur species have been found there.

Currency: Canadian **DOLLAR**

Official languages: **ENGLISH** and **FRENCH**

The **FLOE EDGE** is the location where the frozen ocean meets the open ocean each spring in Nunavut. It is called "the line of life."

National sports: **HOCKEY** and **LACROSSE**

INUIT refers to the people once called Eskimos.

The **JAMES BAY** lies between Quebec and Ontario.

National symbols: **MAPLE LEAF** and **BEAVER**

Government: Constitutional **MONARCHY** (headed by a prime minister)

Highest point: **MOUNT LOGAN**, at 19,551 feet

National anthem: "**O CANADA**"

ONTARIO is Canada's most populated province.

Capital: **OTTAWA**

Churchill is known as the **POLAR BEAR** Capital of the World, because polar bears roam there each winter.

Samuel de Champlain founded **QUEBEC CITY** in 1608.

The **ROGERS PASS**, located in Glacier National Park, links eastern and western Canada.

Canada is the world's **SECOND** largest country in area. *What country is the largest?*

CSA stands for Canadian **SPACE** Agency. That organization manages Canada's space program.

TORONTO is Canada's largest city.

(Largest country in area: **Russia**)

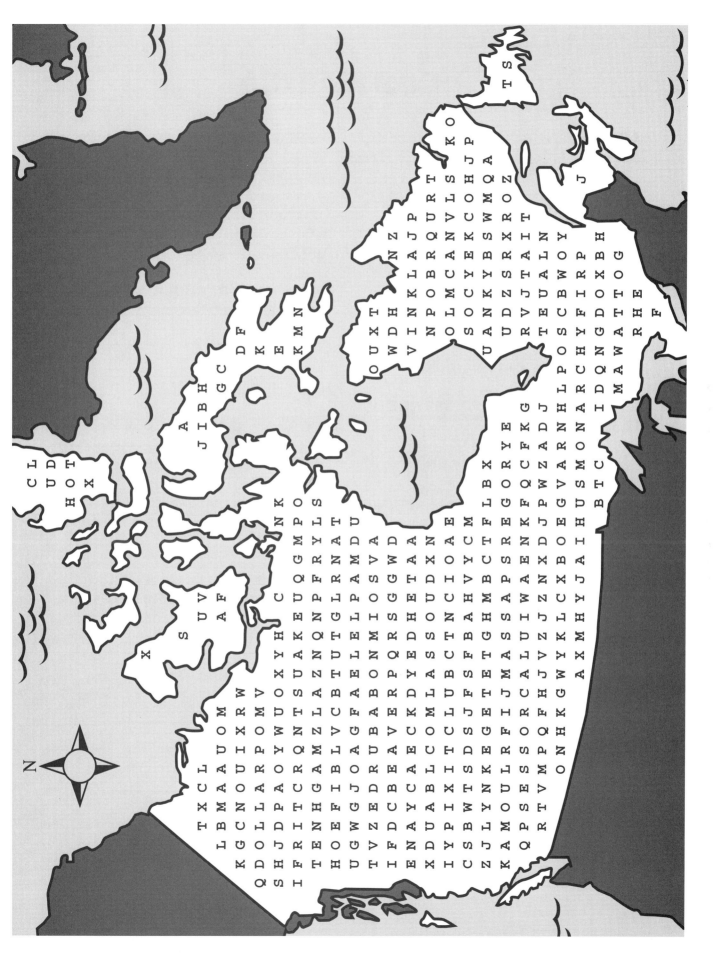

COSTA RICA

ACHIOTE is a fruit used to treat burns and insect bites, as well as to flavor foods.

The **ARENAL** Volcano is Costa Rica's youngest and most active volcano.

BATS make up nearly half of Costa Rica's mammal population.

The Hercules **BEETLE** lives in the forests of Costa Rica.

Official religion: **CATHOLICISM**

Highest point: **CHIRRIPO GRANDE**, at 12,530 feet

Currency: Costa Rican **COLON**

Government: **DEMOCRATIC REPUBLIC** (headed by a Council of Government)

National tree: **GUANACASTE TREE**

HUMPBACK Whales visit Costa Rica twice a year to give birth in the warm waters.

The **IRAZÚ** Volcano is Costa Rica's tallest volcano, at 11,260 feet.

The **POÁS VOLCANO** has the world's second widest crater.

A **PRESIDENT** is the head of state.

National flower: **PURPLE ORCHID**

The crab-eating **RACCOON** can be found in Costa Rica, Panama, and South America.

Official name: **REPÚBLICA DE COSTA RICA**, meaning "Republic of Costa Rica."

Capital: **SAN JOSÉ**

National sport: **SOCCER**

SODAS are small roadside diners.

Official language: **SPANISH**

TAMALES, ground meat and corn meal steamed in banana leaves, are a popular food.

Thousands of the endangered Olive Ridley female **TURTLES** go to Ostional Beach in Tortuguero National Park to lay their eggs.

National bird: **YIGUIRRO**

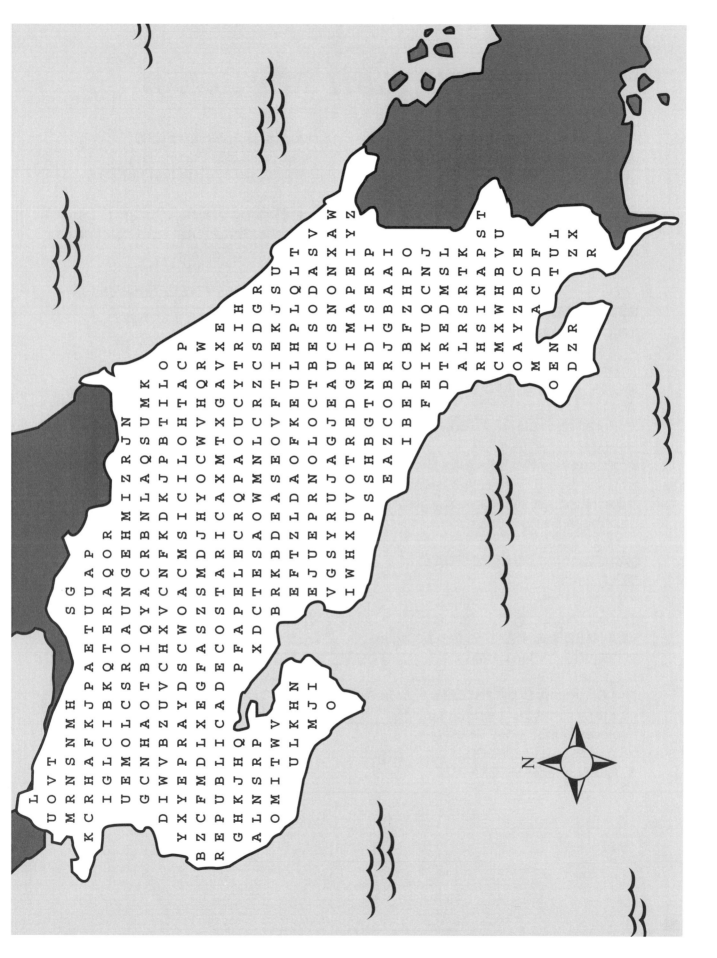

DOMINICAN REPUBLIC

The Dominican Republic covers two thirds of the island of **HISPANIOLA** in the Caribbean.

The **ARTIBONITE** River is Hispaniola's longest river.

National sport: **BASEBALL**

BEACHES are the Dominican Republic's main attractions.

The first building to use mahogany wood was the **CATHEDRAL** of Santo Domingo.

National bird: **COTICA PARROT**

Don't confuse the Dominican Republic, which is part of Hispaniola Island, and **DOMINICA**, an island country in the Caribbean Sea.

Highest point: **DUARTE PEAK**, at 10,417 feet

The world's largest sea turtles, **LEATHERBACK** turtles, can be found here in the national parks.

The Columbus **LIGHTHOUSE** is believed by many to be the resting place of explorer Christopher Columbus.

National dance: **MERENGUE**

Currency: Dominican **PESO**

A **PRESIDENT** is the head of state.

PRIMERO DE MAYO, similar to Labor Day in the United States, is celebrated each year on May 1.

Government: **REPUBLIC** (headed by a president)

Official name: **REPUBLICA** Dominicana, meaning "Dominican Republic."

The endangered **RHINOCEROS IGUANA** can be found here in the national parks.

SANTIAGO is the Dominican Republic's second largest city.

Capital: **SANTO DOMINGO**

The Dominican Republic is the Caribbean's **SECOND** largest country.

Official language: **SPANISH**

The **TAINO** people occupied the Dominican Republic before the Spanish.

The **YAQUE DEL NORTE** River is the Dominican Republic's longest river.

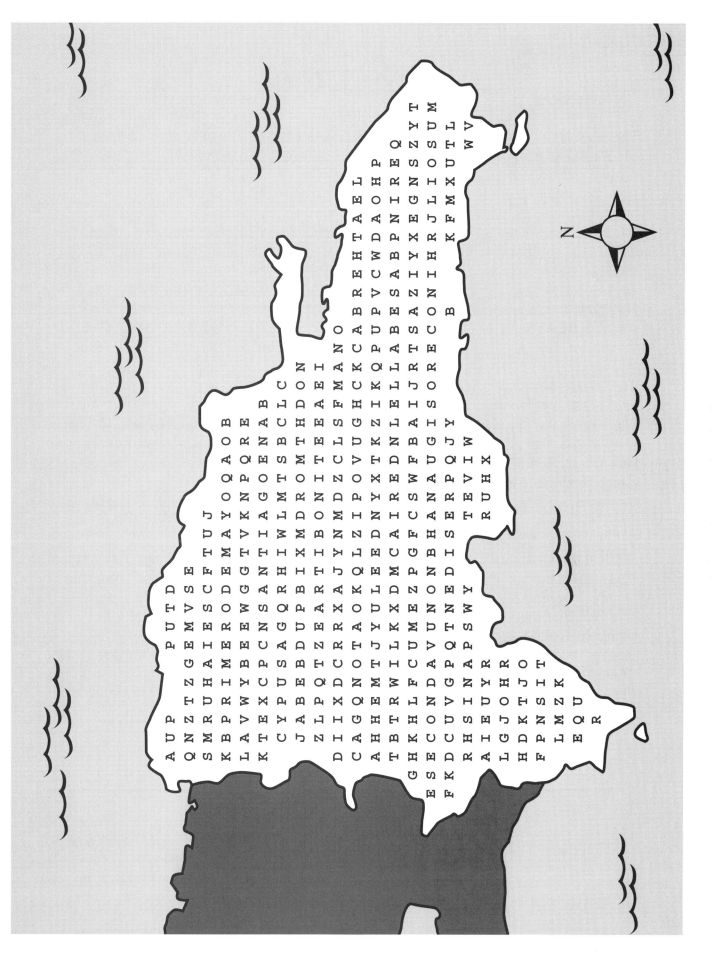

MEXICO

The feast day of de San **ANTONIO** Abad is celebrated every January 17. The Catholic Church opens its doors and allows animals to come in for a blessing.

BAJA California means "Lower California" in Spanish. It is part of Mexico.

Mexico is a world leader for producing **CACAO BEANS**. *What are these beans used to make?*

CINCO DE MAYO is celebrated May 5 each year. It celebrates Mexico's victory over the French in 1862.

DIA DE LOS MUERTOS is celebrated every November 1 and 2 to honor the dead.

Official name: **ESTADOS UNIDOS** Mexicanos, meaning "United Mexican States."

The **GULF** of California separates Baja California from the mainland.

*Cíudad **JUÁREZ** borders which state in the United States?*

LIMEWATER is used to soften corn before it is ground into corn meal.

Capital: **MEXICO CITY**

NOPAL is a native plant. It is a spiky cactus with pear-shaped fruit.

Currency: Mexican New **PESO**

Highest point: **PICO DE ORIZABA**, at 18,410 feet

A **PRESIDENT** is the head of state.

Government: Federal **REPUBLIC** (Each of the 31 states has its own governor and legislature.)

*The river known as the **RIO GRANDE** separates Mexico from which U.S. state?*

A **SOMBRERO** is a felt or straw hat worn by a man to protect himself from the sun.

Official language: **SPANISH**

TLAXCALA is Mexico's smallest state.

The **USUMACINTA** River is Mexico's largest river.

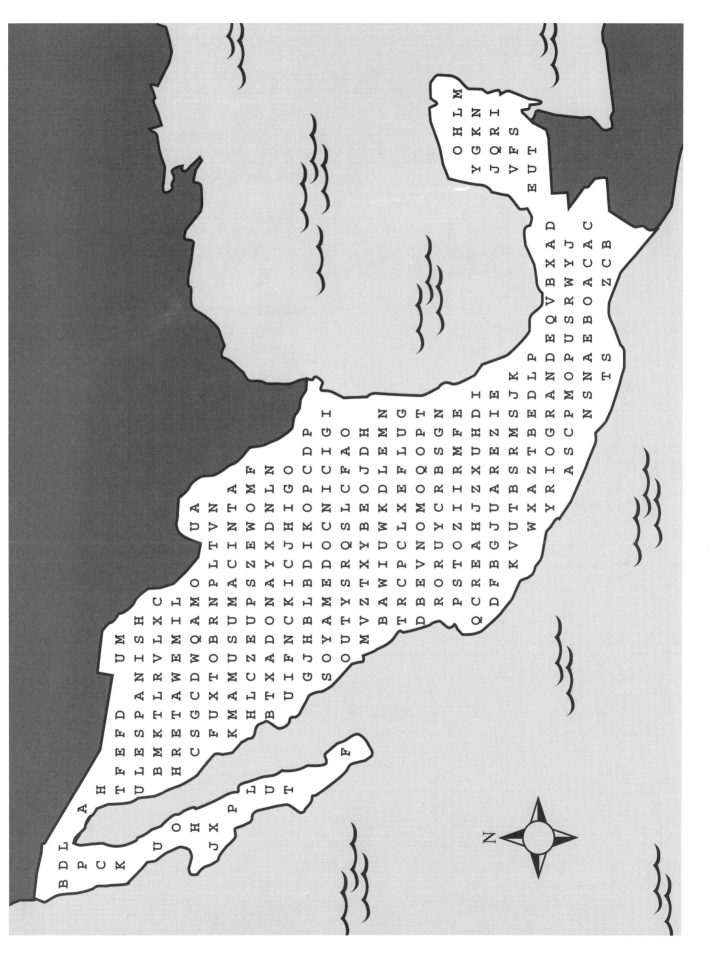

NICARAGUA

For every one hundred people in Nicaragua there is only one **AUTOMOBILE**.

Overripe **BANANAS** are used to make vinegar.

Located in **CARAZO**, La Boquita and Casares are Nicaragua's two most popular beaches.

The **CERRO NEGRO** volcano is Central America's youngest volcano.

COCONUT is an important ingredient in meals on the Caribbean coast.

CORN is used as an ingredient in dishes, drinks, and desserts.

National dish: **GALLO PINTO**. It is a dish of fried rice, onions, peppers, red beans, and garlic.

Currency: **GOLD CORDOBA**

GRANADA is Nicaragua's oldest city.

Ometepe Island is the largest island in **LAKE NICARAGUA**.

Nicaragua is Central America's **LARGEST** country in area.

National tree: **MADROÑO**

Capital: **MANAGUA**

National bird: Turquoise-browed **MOTMOT**

Highest point: **PICO MOGOTÓN**, at 6,913 feet

PLANTAINS are similar to bananas, but much larger, and are a common food in Nicaragua.

Government: **REPUBLIC** (headed by a president)

National flower: **SACUANJOCHE**

SAN CRISTOBAL is Nicaragua's highest active volcano.

SAPODILLAS are sweet fruits, often served after dinner.

Official language: **SPANISH**

TURTLES lay their eggs on the shore of Chacocente Beach.

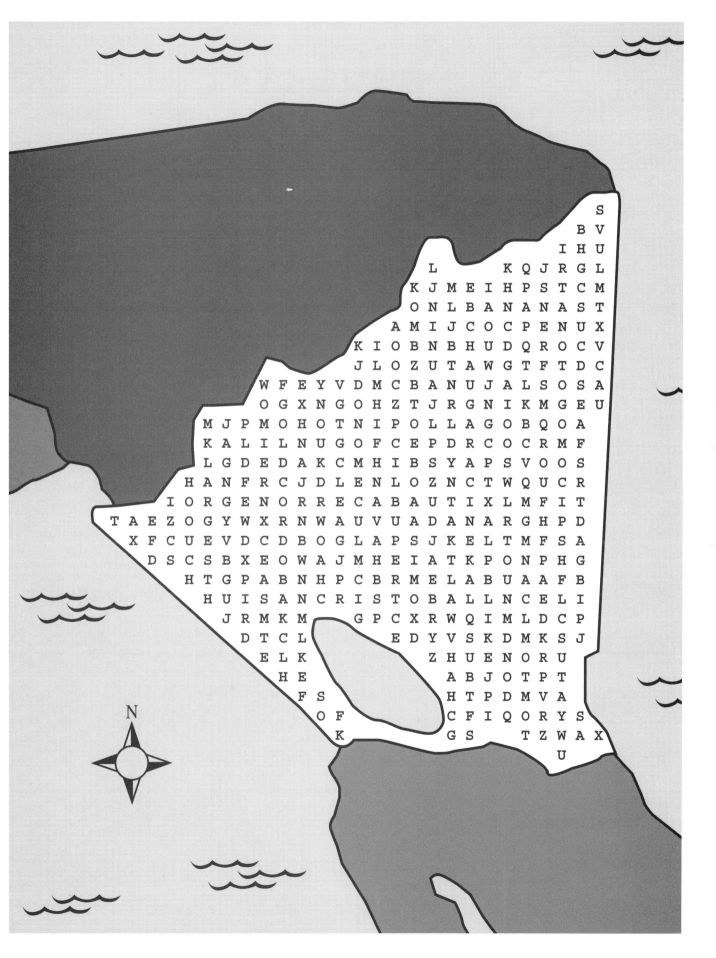

N

```
                                              S
                          B                   V
                          I                   U
                          H                   L
          L         K Q J R G                 L
          K J M E I H P S T C                 M
          O N L B A N A N A S                 T
          A M I J C O C P E N U               X
          K I O B N B H U D Q R O C           V
          J L O Z U T A W G T F T D           C
      W F E Y V D M C B A N U J A L S O S     A
      O G X N G O H Z T J R G N I K M G E     U
  M J P M O H O T N I P O L L A G O B Q O     A
  K A L I L N U G O F C E P D R C O C R M     F
  L G D E D A K C M H I B S Y A P S V O O     S
  H A N F R C J D L E N L O Z N C T W Q U C   R
  I O R G E N O R R E C A B A U T I X L M F I T
T A E Z O G Y W X R N W A U V U A D A N A R G H P D
X F C U E V D C D B O G L A P S J K E L T M F S A
D S C S B X E O W A J M H E I A T K P O N P H G
H T G P A B N H P C B R M E L A B U A A F B
H U I S A N C R I S T O B A L L N C E L I
J R M K M       G P C X R W Q I M L D C P
D T C L         E D Y V S K D M K S J
E L K           Z H U E N O R U
H E             A B J O T P T
F S             H T P D M V A
O F             C F I Q O R Y S
K               G S       T Z W A X
                            U
```

PANAMA

Currency: **BALBOA**

BASEBALL is a popular sport in Panama.

CASH CROPS, such as bananas, are grown to sell.

The **CHAGRES** River pours into the Gatun Lake, which is part of the Panama Canal.

Panama gained its independence from **COLOMBIA** in 1903.

COLÓN is one of Panama's largest cities.

The **GATUN** Lake is Panama's largest and only lake.

GAUCHO is a dish of mixed rice and beans.

The **ISTHMUS OF PANAMA** is a strip of land that separates the Caribbean Sea and the Pacific Ocean.

The United States built the **PANAMA CANAL** through the Isthmus of Panama, to shorten the travel distance between San Francisco and New York. It was completed in 1914.

Capital: **PANAMA CITY**

Government: **REPUBLIC** (headed by a president)

Official name: **REPÚBLICA** de Panama, meaning "Republic of Panama."

Children have to attend school and complete at least the **SIXTH GRADE**.

Official language: **SPANISH**

SQUATTERS are people who live and farm on government or private land they do not own.

The **STRAW HATS** that farmers wear are not the famous Panama hats. *Where do Panama hats come from?*

SUBSISTENCE crops, such as rice, are grown for the farmers' use.

Of Panama's 500 rivers, only the **TUIRA** River is navigable.

Highest point: **VOLCÁN BARÚ**, at 11,401 feet

(Country where Panama hats originate: **Ecuador**)

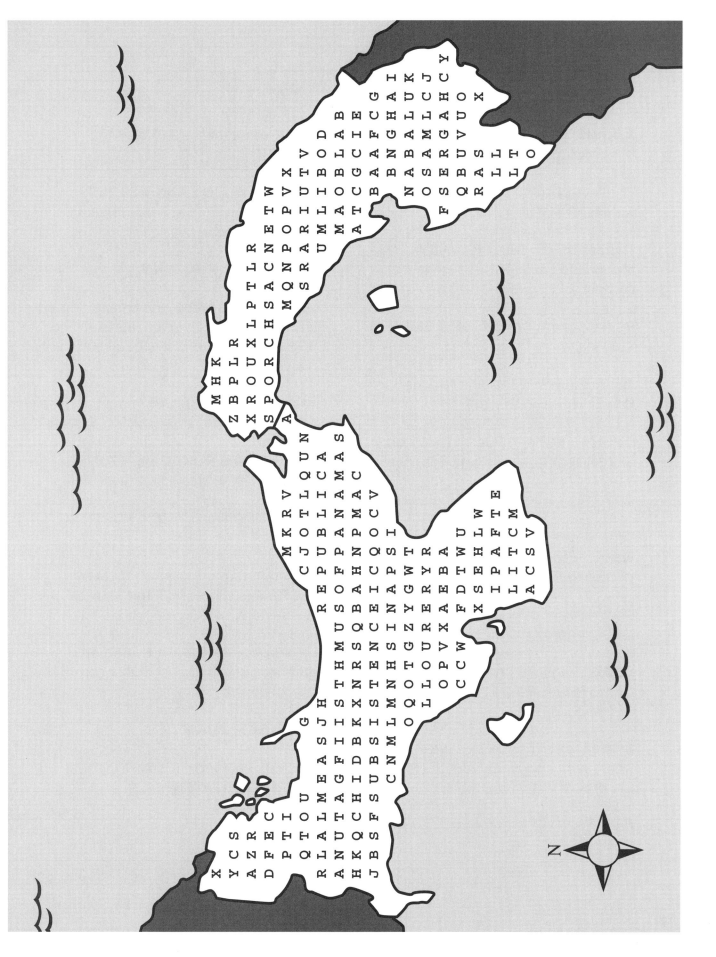

PUERTO RICO

ADJUNTAS has an average yearly temperature of 72 degrees Fahrenheit.

The **ARECIBO** Observatory holds the world's largest single-dish radio telescope.

The beaches in **BARCELONETA** have black sand because it is high in iron content.

Highest point: **CERRO DE PUNTA**, at 4,389 feet

The president of the United States is Puerto Rico's **CHIEF OF STATE**.

CIDRA is home to Puerto Rico's only blue-eyed bird, La Paloma Sabanera.

COFFEE is Puerto Rico's main crop.

Official name: Estado Libre Asociado de Puerto Rico, meaning "**COMMONWEALTH** of Puerto Rico."

Government: **CONGRESS** (headed by the U.S. Congress and an elected governor)

COQUI frogs are brown and are one inch to two inches long. They are native to Puerto Rico.

CUEVA DEL INDIO is a cave in Arecibo where native carvings from the Prehistoric Era are carved on the walls.

Currency: United States **DOLLAR**

Official languages: **ENGLISH** and **SPANISH**

The **FESTIVAL DE LAS FLORES**, meaning "Flowers Festival," is held each year in Aibonito.

Official flower: **HIBISCUS**

ISLA DEL ENCANTO, the phrase printed on the U.S. 2009 quarter representing Puerto Rico, means "Isle of Enchantment" in Spanish.

Puerto Rico is an **ISLAND** *in the Caribbean Sea that sits closest to which U.S. state?*

In 1509, **JUAN PONCE DE LEON** became Puerto Rico's first governor.

Puerto Rico means "**RICH PORT**" in Spanish.

Located in Camuy, the **RIO CAMUY** Cave Park is the world's third largest cave system.

The Arecibo **RIVER** is one of Puerto Rico's longest rivers used for hydro-electric power.

Capital: **SAN JUAN**

Residents of Puerto Rico are citizens of the **UNITED STATES**.

(U.S. state closest to Puerto Rico: **Florida**)

```
  T L C
  X M U X W B P A Q   B T L P       P U E
  V C E G C O N G R E S S E C R A M D T V F T V C S     R K F
H A K V T U C O N B C C S E R O L F S A L E D L A V I T S E F R S
U H T L A E W N O M M O C R F T B C R O F W S G N U D E N G L I S H C H U
M E A D V Y L M Q D E R G F D A I N G X Y R J H D E J Z Y C E F J S T M
  N B E Z S K E R U O D F O G O T H A A Z U X I W F R U H B D K I H I Y
  O R L B A F J Z D I K H C C B I S R E A I H B T S Q P N C D N E F A
  L I I S L A D E L E N C A N T O E D N J C H I E F O F S T A T E
  E C N V R G P S G F M M C U A C A I E K Q Y S S R P A X P A L M
D C H D M E U Y X J H U F R X I J S C L T P B C T L O W S K T S
K R G I N N R T I K Y L U Z B K L B D N M I Z U I R A L L O D U
E A J O T O H U J U A N P O N C E D E L E O N S I U N N B C U
L B F A Q P V W         Q M     R C O   A K U L M V   D O
```

N

UNITED STATES OF AMERICA

ALASKA is the United States' largest state in surface area.

National bird: **BALD EAGLE**

The **BLUE RIDGE MOUNTAINS** extend from Pennsylvania to Georgia.

The **CONSTITUTION** was written in 1787.

Lowest point: **DEATH VALLEY** at 282 feet below sea level. *In which state is this desert located?*

Currency: U.S. **DOLLAR**

Chief language: **ENGLISH**

The three branches of the U.S. government are the **EXECUTIVE**, **JUDICIARY**, and the **LEGISLATIVE**.

The **FIRST AMENDMENT** of the Constitution allows Americans freedom of religion and freedom of speech.

The **GRAND CANYON** is located in Arizona.

People naturally float in the **GREAT SALT LAKE** because the water is high in salt content.

The state of **HAWAII** is a group of islands that lies in the Pacific Ocean. The island of Hawaii is the United States' largest island.

At 22,300 square miles, Lake **MICHIGAN** is the United States' largest lake.

At 2,565 miles long, the **MISSOURI** River is the United States' longest river.

Highest point: **MOUNT MCKINLEY**, at 20,320 feet. *In which state is this mountain located?*

The **PLEDGE OF ALLEGIANCE** is a promise of loyalty. ("I pledge allegiance to the flag . . . ")

Government: **REPUBLIC** (headed by a president)

National flower: **ROSE**

The United States is the world's **THIRD** most populous country.

Official name: **UNITED STATES OF AMERICA**

Capital: **WASHINGTON, D.C.**

(U.S. state in which Mt. McKinley is located: **Alaska**)
(U.S. state in which Death Valley is located: **California**)

SOUTH AMERICA

Highest point in South America: **ACONCAGUA** in Argentina, at 22,835 feet

The **AMAZON RIVER BASIN** is the world's second longest river.

ANACONDA is the name of a group of snakes in South America that can grow up to 30 feet long and weigh as much as 450 pounds.

The **ANDES MOUNTAINS**, which stretch over 4,500 miles, are the world's second highest mountain range. *What is the name of the highest mountain in the world, and where it is located?*

The **ATACAMA DESERT** in Chile is one of Earth's driest places.

Related to the camel, the alpaca can be found in Peru and **BOLIVIA**.

BRAZIL is South America's largest country in area and in population.

*The **CROW** can be found in all of the continents except South America and which other continent?*

CURARE is a poisonous substance that native people placed on their arrows to kill animals.

The earth's equator runs through **ECUADOR**.

Several explorers went to South America in search of a wealthy fictional kingdom called **EL DORADO**.

At 6,887,000 square miles, South America is the world's **FOURTH** largest continent in area.

The **IVORY PALM** is a tree native to South America.

LAKE MARACAIBO is South America's largest lake. *Where is it located?*

LLANOS are grassy plains that are good for cattle ranching.

PARAGUAY is a landlocked country located between Brazil and Argentina.

The **PARANÁ RIVER** is South America's second longest river.

PERU is home to Machu Picchu, a royal palace in the Andes Mountains.

The **QUINOA** plant is native to the Andes Mountains.

SURINAME is South America's smallest independent country in area and population.

VENEZUELA is home to the world's highest waterfall, Angel Falls.

YANOMAMI INDIANS live in Brazil's rain forests.

(Country in which Lake Maracaibo is located: **Venezuela**)

(Continent other than South America where the crow can't be found: **Antarctica**)

(Highest mountain in the world: **Mt. Everest, in Tibet and Nepal**)

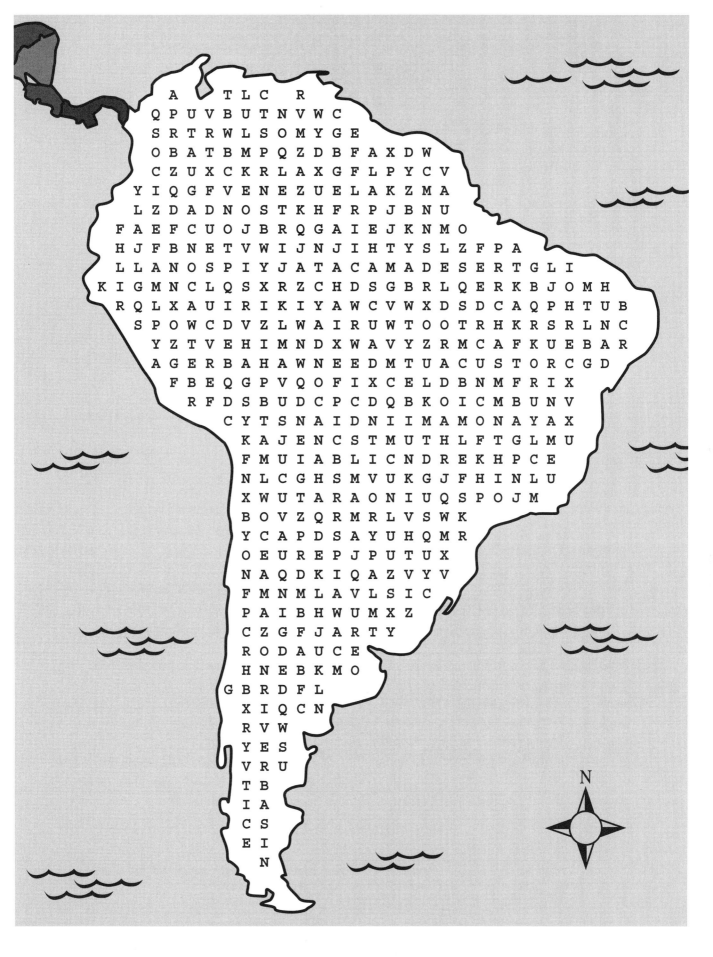

ARGENTINA

Highest point: **ACONCAGUA**, at 22,835 feet. It is the Western Hemisphere's tallest mountain.

AGOUTIS are two-footed rodents living in the thick forests of Argentina.

The **ANDES** *Mountains separate Argentina from which other South American country?*

The classic way to cook meat here is on an **ASADO**, also known as a barbecue.

Capital: **BUENOS AIRES**

CÓRDOBA is Argentina's second largest city.

Argentina is the world's **EIGHTH** largest country in area.

A **GAUCHO** is a cowboy who drives cattle in the Pampas.

The **GUANACO** is a relative of the camel. It can be found here.

IGUAÇU FALLS is made up of 275 individual waterfalls that fall at the border of Argentina and Brazil.

The dried leaves from a **MATE PLANT** are used to make a high caffeine tea.

The **MONKEY PUZZLE** Tree is native to the Andes Mountains.

PAMPAS means "plains" in Spanish. It is the name given to describe the open grassland region.

One of the world's oldest dinosaurs, *Euroraptor*, was found in **PATAGONIA**.

Currency: Argentine **PESO**

A **PONCHO** is a blanket with a hole in the center that slips over the head.

Government: **REPUBLIC** (headed by a president)

Official name: **REPÚBLICA** Argentina, meaning "Argentine Republic."

Argentina is South America's **SECOND** largest country in area.

Official language: **SPANISH**

The **SUPERCLASICO** is the annual football (soccer) game between Argentina's two most popular teams, Boca Juniors and River Plate.

National music and dance: **TANGO**

TIERRA DEL FUEGO is known as "The End of the World."

USHUAIA is the world's southernmost city and is located on the island of Tierra Del Fuego.

(Country separated from Argentina by the Andes Mountains: **Chile**)

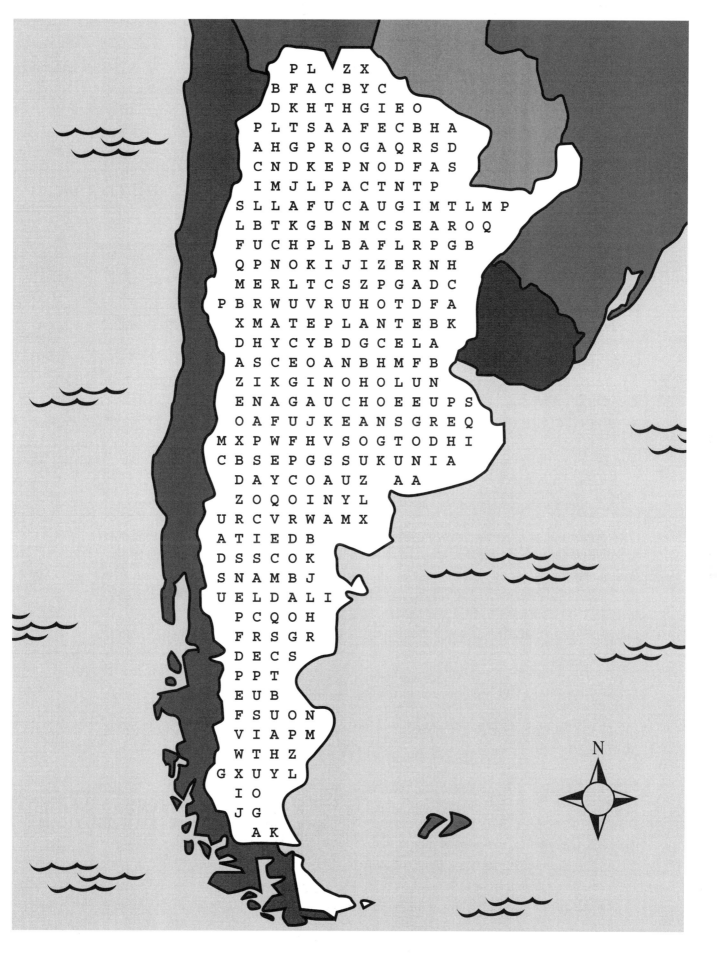

BRAZIL

The **AMAZON** rain forest is the largest tropical rain forest in the world.

Brazil is one of the world's leading makers of **AUTOMOBILES**.

BOMBACHAS are baggy trousers worn by gauchos.

Capital: **BRASÍLIA**

Violin bows are made from **BRAZILWOOD** trees that grow here.

A martial art known as **CAPOEIRA** developed in Brazil in the 1500s.

Similar in appearance to a beaver, the **CAPYBARA** is the world's largest rodent. It can weigh up to 100 pounds!

CARNIVAL is a four-day colorful festival celebrated before Lent.

At 2,330 feet above sea level, the statue **CHRIST THE REDEEMER** overlooks the city of Rio de Janeiro and the harbor.

Brazil produces more **COFFEE** than any other country in the world.

Brazil is the world's **FIFTH** most populated country.

FOOTBALL (soccer) is Brazil's favorite sport.

The **GE INDIANS** are one of Brazil's largest tribes living in the central region.

Brazil is South America's **LARGEST** country in area and in population.

Highest point: **PICO DA NEBLINA**, at 9,888 feet

Official language: **PORTUGUESE**

Currency: **REAL**

Government: Federal **REPUBLIC** (headed by a president)

Official name: **REPÚBLICA** Federativa Do Brasil, meaning "Federative Republic of Brasil."

RIO DE JANEIRO is a popular vacation and tourist spot.

The **SÃO FRANCISCO** River, located in the east, flows through Brazil and empties into the Atlantic Ocean.

SÃO PAULO is one of the world's most populous cities.

Rural families that live near the river build their houses on **STILTS** to avoid floods.

The **TAPIOCA** starch that comes from the roots of a cassava plant is used to make pudding.

Located in Amapa, **TUMUCUMAQUE** National Park is the largest tropical forest park in the world.

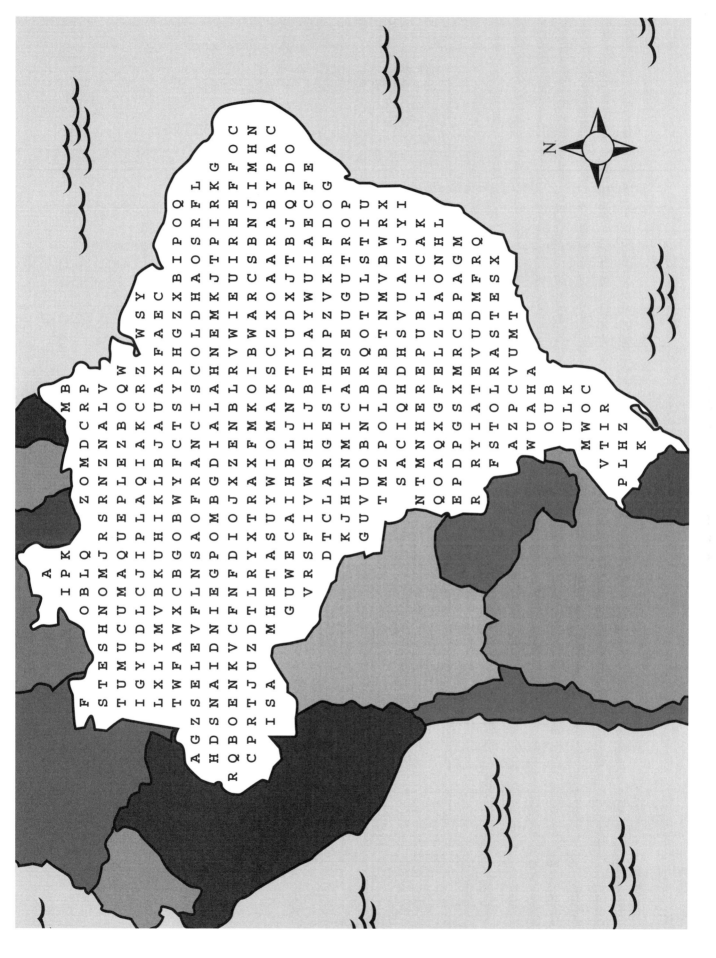

COLOMBIA

AGUA DE PANELA is a drink made of brown sugar and water.

National bird: **ANDEAN CONDOR**

Bogotá has Latin America's largest organization of **BICYCLE LANES**.

Capital: **BOGOTÁ**

National flower: **CATTLEYA TRIANAE ORCHID**

COFFEE is Colombia's most important crop.

Highest point: Pico **CRISTÓBAL COLÓN**, at 18,947 feet

Traditional music genre: **CUMBIA**

The **EQUATOR** runs through the city of Caqueta.

GORGONA ISLAND became a national park in 1985.

The **HARPY EAGLE** lives here. On average, it weighs ten pounds and stands three feet tall.

The Amacayacu National Natural Park is home to the world's smallest primate, the black-faced **LION MARMOSET**.

MALPELO ISLAND is a rocky island in the Pacific Ocean. It is visited by many birds, fish, and sharks.

NEVADO DEL RUIZ is an active volcano.

Colombia is South America's only country to have both the Atlantic and Pacific **OCEANS** touching its coastline.

The **ORINOCO RIVER** forms a borderline between Colombia and Venezuela.

National tree: **PALMA DE CERA**

Currency: Colombian **PESO**

Government: **REPUBLIC** (headed by a president)

Official name: **REPÚBLICA** de Colombia, meaning "Republic of Colombia."

A **RUANA** is a blanket with a slit in the middle for the head.

SANTA MARTA is South America's oldest city.

SOCCER is Colombia's most popular spectator sport.

Official language: **SPANISH**

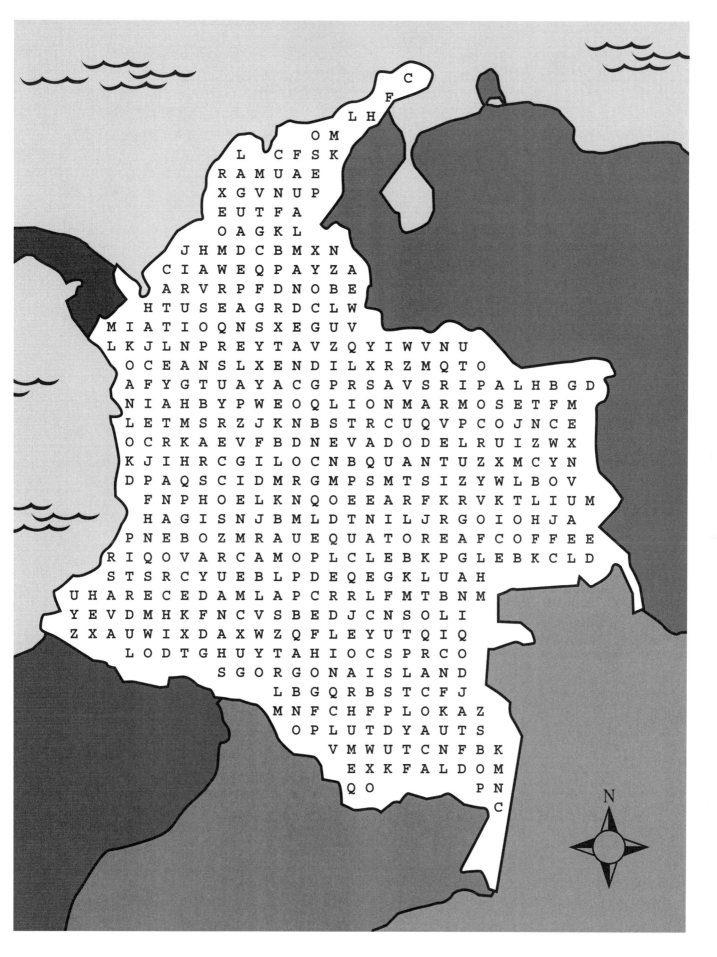

ECUADOR

The **ANDES HIGHLAND** is also known as the Sierra.

Ecuador is the world's leading **BALSA WOOD** producer.

The **CERO LATITUD** Film Festival takes place every October in Quito.

Highest point: **CHIMBORAZO VOLCANO**, at 20,702 feet

The **CINCHONA** plant, used to treat malaria, was first found in Ecuador and one other country. *What was that country?*

At 19,347 feet, **COTOPAXI** is one of the world's highest active volcanoes.

Panama hats are produced in **CUENCA**.

The large, female **CURASSOW** bird lives in the forest, and lays two eggs at a time!

Ecuador is a Spanish word for "**EQUATOR**."

A monument marks the center of the earth's surface, 0° −0′ −0″ latitude, located in the **EQUINOCTIAL ANDES**.

The **GALAPAGOS ISLANDS** are a province of Ecuador.

GUAYAQUIL is Ecuador's largest city.

LLOA is home to Ecuador's active twin-cratered volcano, Guagua **PICHINCHA**.

MINDO is one of the world's best spots for bird watching.

The **ORIENTE** region is the Eastern Lowland that consists of tropical forests and rivers.

Capital: **QUITO**

Government: **REPUBLIC** (headed by a president)

Official name: **REPÚBLICA** del Ecuador, meaning "Republic of Ecuador."

National anthem: "**SALVE, O PATRIA**," meaning "Hail, O Fatherland."

Official language: **SPANISH**

The Sierra has **SPRINGLIKE** weather all year round.

Currency: **U.S. DOLLAR**

A **WAHOO** is a pointed-nosed fish that can grow up to six feet long.

(Country other than Ecuador where the cinchona was first found: **Peru**)

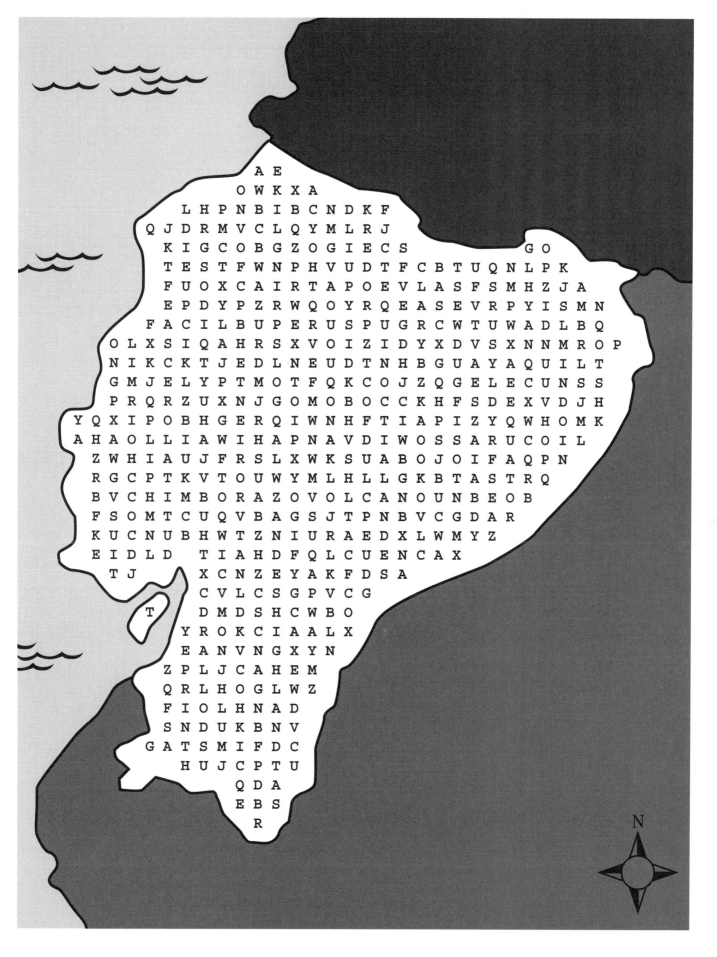

VENEZUELA

ANGEL FALLS is the world's highest waterfall.

National tree: **ARAGUANEY**

AREPA is a traditional cornmeal bread.

Currency: **BOLIVAR FUERTE**

Official name: República **BOLIVARIANA** de Venezuela, meaning "Bolivarian Republic of Venezuela."

Capital: **CARACAS**

CIUDAD BOLIVAR is Venezuela's major shipping port.

A **CUATRO** is a four-string guitar.

National anthem: "**GLORIA AL BRAVO PUEBLO**," meaning "Glory to the Brave People."

GUACHAROS are large birds that live mainly in the Cave of the Guacharo in Caripe.

The **GURI DAM** is one of the world's largest dams.

National dish: **HALLACA**

National folk dance: **JOROPO**

LAKE MARACAIBO is South America's largest lake.

Venezuela means "**LITTLE VENICE**" in Spanish.

LLANEROS are the cowboys hired to work ranches.

National flower: Venezuelan **ORCHID**

The **ORINOCO** River is Venezuela's longest river.

PARIMA-TAPIRAPECO is Venezuela's largest national park.

Highest point: **PICO BOLÍVAR**, at 16,411 feet

Government: Federal **REPUBLIC** (headed by a president)

Venezuela is South America's **SIXTH** largest country.

Venezuela gained its full independence from **SPAIN** in 1821.

Official language: **SPANISH**

National bird: **TURPIAL**

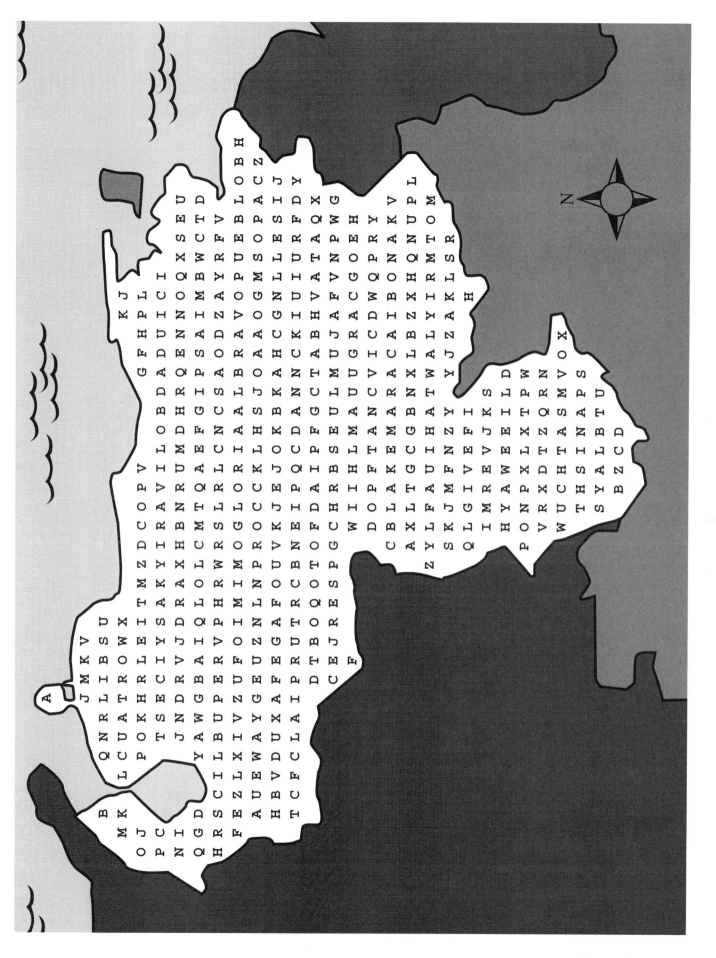

AFRICA

```
                S K P V
            F K L Z E U A D
            A Y C M D M S W C R        F
          T J X O K J Z A B H (S O M A L I A) T V Z
        U O M W L T C F T X D M S N B I G E U S A A I
        T A I V R E N B Y L (G A B O N) J H S U F I Y W
      K V I N W A D G I S R F L G Q A H D T P R P X H J
      L (E W B A B M I Z) H S A V M L A T I C R E G O F Q P
      P Z C N H U J V Q A N O W A K K S R Q G X C I R L K O
      Q B D P O T B O P I Q M U P O I Z C L Q Z E H T W V Y N
      R A M E G C H I K U Y L T T J Y L A A B D B T M U Z X I
      Z C N B S I G R V T X N K B H N Y M F R A M E U A O L K J
      D L G F D U E Q S Z O C I (M A U R I T I U S) T S M B T A S
      A J C O (B U R U N D I) R C H G F N K Z D A C B H N D I R Y U      A V
      H Q E L F E R W O P X D N N X R E P H E L G P O N H J Z A X I W
        D R    A    (K E N Y A) W O I K R I F Q D A S M C D U B E
                G T C D C C B S T E Z R Q O N P M O I
                Q E V I L E A N M (N I G E R I A) L
                F K P B R W F L A O U S F H Z N
                R A U I V F W T I E Q F P O M
                E L A Q O P A P N L G R E U L
                S T A X L M L O A S T I K
                S R N T K P A R H D J U
                Z T U V D J Q R E I A C
                (N U L N I C R E (T P Y G E)
                I Y O H G S E I Y N W S B
                V G (C O M O R O S) X Z E A V
                M E M K L I H F Q P L U C S
                S R X O P C T R B L O T
                W A T R E U S E N T L
                P I O D O V H N L M C
                M C X W C K I J F
                A Y Z Y H C N
                B A E D C I O
                (S U D A N)
                G F E B
```

EGYPT

```
        A S F L U                A W N A F U X                C
        T D H M V A C R A R      C X U M V P S M S T U M X V R
        G W U A X S Q P V W X D T V T S O B P L C E X T M L H
        B X R G W L U S T Y B U S I L M H C N I S M A H K C J
    U Y H E P O A P S U Q O Z D C V P T A H Z T      F R I B R
      V (M O D G N I K D E T I N U) R K I Y R B A        Z X R U Z
      C Z Q F S H G F B P S E A E W R T I R K M U        E H D
      C P D T I O T I R P R E B O Q L B A T E A L        T U R
      I J F M G B C K O A Z S P Q J M A C S H T W          R
      R E A G H N U C D C X U K X U C R L R T S P M
      P D J B D V A N O N F R A P I H A C U A V C L T
      J O H K A M E H N I (A Y Y I B A L A G M) B A H A
      B C K M M L J D J M N P Z O R L A D H C D E F G C
      X N I L A D K M L E M A L N H K R K B P G S T I H E
      U B M C B L W A K H V P U A B X (S Q A R O U N) H C R
      L O N U K L P L T B G F Y M G R I C E M W U R K M K J
      A T H A J X E C R U V W Y S C M A I A L X D S U A H
      G P G I Y K X K G I X T B U V T R S H Z B T N X L B
      N S V Z H J A V A F N W L T S A E T C P Y J K Z T T M B
      I Q F J I U N J F H G A C P T Y I E J K Y F E R S N D K
      T X W Y A Z D U T S L S H F G I U O L H G L Q D U (E L I N)
      I R E K H S R M E D I D K Z R F A I D X I G P B M O N L I
      (R E P U B L I C) J I N M Z E U U P V M N (D N U O P) N Z M V N O
      W V D Y G T A I X L K E J Y H R Z H O W I G H R R R E A H V
      Z M L V R B E R (R A S M O H A M E D) P E J F A E V E F S X Q P
      Q C U W C A F L C U H J A I X U C H G Q W B X D V I Q R T U
      N R T C F E M H D B N R F D V J W K R T K L C S W O Q H W
      P B V X D (V E I L) E Q O B H K L P U S F U M E U V G P R
      A O S D E F G T D A I P G C W (Q A T T A R A) O S
```

ETHIOPIA

B A R T I X U S
X S Q R F T U X Z V N T X
R P E V A C R A M O F O S A
Z T O T P S R Z S T B D U T U
Q R S U R U D A X E U P R L Z
Y R N O R D M E A C R J M K V E A
F I P M P Q A S U F S S A I L B P
K B L X U S M O H L M N H M C Q O R
M U G O L I W K V S A S A E H N Z A
E S A I N T M A R Y T D M O N P G Y R
J T H T N V B T S B R G P M G A T S B F H Y
D S E C H A K L E A X B H E A R X W E G H E R
N U I R V X J U W D Z F U Q L M F D C R X S Z Q
A V W O U M W E A C E V E I F V U T I L A G I S J
D N D W J B I N V F L Q A M H A R I C K D R P K D L
O P A K C L A I R D N M C D V L F J Q C T E A O I C O M N
G T C T K R Y L W M E P O R D U E M U B T A B Y S S I N I A S F
L F T C S L S E T G E N N A N W X C I N K P K W T U T N I V L E U E Y L X Z R P
K P U B J Z K H F T L F D C D Y K S J L A L R E G U H Q C B T C E O U L A
M L N M D J A A X E D O M S B T D A O M U I E V M E X K R U I U A V M
I Q R A G R L P H K A E E Z J E M B V B F K W T W R J L C P B S T
A N I Y F L Y V L H X T A S R I V A T T X O F D C A S T L E S
P E H Z S L U C S B L J I C N W S B V C J Y S D I S U P H R
O A B N O I S S E R P E D L I K A N A D Y G C Q P M A U K
G E B F K L R F U Z C H O W B R L Z I Z F H L T V M
C Q U E T P A Y I F H B G Z U Q L A E H B
F O D M L U M J V Y V Q P T Y P E D A
H T G Z W G U A F X O R Y C
F K A H X M

KENYA

S T M L U P K H E G Q
Z P A W X O Z W N F B C C U V
L V U T K I S S I C R M D H H M H F S I J
A Q H A P G O L J I K V J P T K R B E A T O L
S Z M Y T B F L N O X M W U E L S Q E X L C D A S G Q M
R B X C U N I T E D K I N G D O M S M K H G I A I M
A T H I U H N Y L T G U E A Z R F D W R L N B O
W D V E A S Z M S L D P B X F T V S X A O P M L
C G F E J N P E I R H N G M H A C B R Z Y B O U
G E C D Q A R S W C V G S D B U C O D P Z T M X
D I O A K Y H L J I O C R G P R T I A R F E A Z
H B N L P N K Y X F E P O Q L S Q C L E R D B P
C A M N Z E V M G T D B O R A J N A M I L I K O
V A W O X T K G Q S U O D L P K U B P E Z H F U Z
B U P H J R A P S O R M N Q F M S M O E A R U A C E
F Q C Z V Y O X S R W O V E A T J N T P G Z F M Y W M
C X T X J P T B O T U H S M E R O U L N K D H W X D S
R B G R L A G A W A N A T W E R I J P V G N L Q I X B P
Z D S N U F B U V T H C I X F B D S T N A H P E L E P Q
I N H Q K U I Q Y Z O S E H R L M O N P D Z A S
E M C O E C T U J A R L Z X R E T H G L Q E W J R
D C L I P N J H N J P I C G T G C R A S I M R B H P O
K J O Y D A J V B A T H I J Y Q K Y J K C T E Z R W
A E R G D M N Y A F Y U F G H N T H K U E U V N T
F I K Z N O U V K I Z R F E J U I V S Y I X A U
W A X T Q Z G W E L A K E V I C T O R I A M
L M B E H J C A E U A O U T H Z I O K
L F O S S I L S Y V N S M G F J L
K C N D L T I P W R Y B C
I M U T B R B Q X A A E
H C F A U G E L R D
W V K H P H B K J
B X Z M F E I B
D S A Z A R C
U Y J R M Z
M L U V
X

MOROCCO

```
                       L
                    S  R  A
                    V  U  A  B  K
                    L  C  I  G  I  B  R  Q  M  S  P
                 P  I  Z  S  J  C  O  U  S  C  O  U  S  O
                 D  B  X  A  S  C  K  V  L  O  U  T  N  F  E  X
              A  Y  F  E  O  D  H  W  X  C  T  S  D  N  R  Z
              R  V  Z  L  A  U  T  B  I  M  X  C  L  I  L  U  P
           U  O  A  H  A  S  S  A  N  I  I  M  O  S  Q  U  E  V  S  U
        Z  J  H  M  X  W  A  Z  B  H  H  I  G  R  Q  T  M  O  Y  X  B  T  W
     A  H  N  O  A  V  Z  S  R  T  A  O  U  I  J  V  H  A  B  A  L  L  E  J
  G  C  M  I  B  L  Y  V  C  A  L  P  T  L  B  H  P  R  R  T  E  A  U  T  J
     E  T  A  H  P  S  O  H  P  L  H  U  I  J  R  K  A  S  K  L  U  O  X  V  H
     K  F  J  B  S  U  I  M  U  A  N  V  A  S  L  A  K  O  B  E  R  B  E  R  S  U  O
           S  E  L  C  R  T  A  Z  X  D  P  O  M  W  R  H  L  S  N  V  T  U
        J  A  N  D  Q  P  S  R  B  B  M  L  Q  I  X  G  A  T  M
     F  M  O  O  R  E  G  R  A  L  E  N  O  N  Z  Y  F  A  E
     G  B  I  E  K  D  U  O  N  K  D  A  K  J  T  S  B  A  R  A
     C  H  D  L  H  J  I  B  M  T  F  E  N  I  T  B  A  C  D
        F  M  R  Z  K  I  B  L  U  C  B  G  C  E  R
     I  N  M  X  S  E  T  A  R  I  P  A  H  A
     S  O  D  I  U  M  P  T  S  O  H  J
  Y  H  C  R  A  N  O  M
     O  A  H  D  M  L
     P  M  A  I  V  U
     I  M  I  T  C
  U  R  Q  E  U  T  L  T
  T  V  E  D  I  R  H  A  M
S  W  X  A  V  Z  Y  O  U  S  Z
```

ANTARCTICA

```
                    L  P  T  S  K
                    R  Z  C  A  B  U  F  H  P
                 Z  L  X  B  D  G  A  M  Q  F  H  T  M  U
              K  Y  C  W  H  D  Q  O  E  G  L  S  Y  A  X
              A  J  Z  M  V  N  U  E  R  K  R  S  I  N  Z  B  W  K  J
              B  C  I  A  U  N  T  S  F  Q  J  P  E  O  C  V  L  C  N  O  T  V
              Y  T  A  E  R  T  C  I  T  C  R  A  T  N  A  W  C  P  E  I  D  S
              S  K  N  B  E  A  I  T  U  V  B  C  Q  L  P  I  U  M  Q  H  R  X
              T  E  H  R  L  V  T  D  L  A  U  W  V  X  W  O  C  B  G  D  G  J  Y
  T           U  I  C  E  X  T  M  C  K  C  M  R  I  X  R  V  Y  N  E  C  I  Z  H  I
  L  C        M  D  O  R  B  A  U  K  E  R  D  S  Q  N  I  Y  P  S  U  C  F  A  M  K  C  L
  F  E        C  F  L  C  D  M  J  F  R  U  C  U  R  Q  W  B  Y  A  T  C  G  R  Z  C  F  O  A  T  Z  X  Z  E  A
  K  A  E      M  R  O  S  S  I  C  E  S  H  E  L  F  J  E  T  N  P  B  Q  M  X  E  D  S  U  L  P  S  F  U
  C  F  L  C  D  M  J  B  A  W  E  X  L  I  V  S  P  E  V  Z  I  N  D  O  S  A  W  Y  S  B  T  K  J  H  E  B  H  G
              L  K  S  V  A  H  Y  I  D  U  G  A  F  K  A  Q  T  L  V  Z  E  U  S  R  N  E  P  A  Q  B  R  C  S
              F  T  W  J  M  Y  X  N  T  O  F  J  G  H  S  E  N  U  A  S  V  C  R  M  E  O  Z  L  F  K  E  K  I  P
              D  M  F  O  U  P  G  J  S  N  C  G  B  I  F  N  C  B  I  S  Z  Y  H  X  T  W  A  G  V  M  U  H  R  T  J
              S  T  L  R  I  F  Z  V  O  S  T  O  K  S  T  A  T  I  O  N  K  I  G  S  Y  X  Q  K  V  P  U  O  I  S  N
              F  Q  R  A  C  B  M  S  K  N  G  O  I  H  B  D  R  C  M  A  J  G  Y  F  X  R  Y  S  W  E  A  T  Z  L  G  B
  D           H  O  N  A  E  T  M  N  C  U  F  E  C  T  E  I  O  F  L  H  O  A  Y  I  Y  E  Z  R  E  I  L  F  A
              P  C  T  L  R  V  A  E  F  G  T  K  G  F  J  Q  T  M  E  Z  B  Z  J  C  O  L  D  E  S  T  B  Z  C
              G  Q  B  U  D  W  S  L  A  H  D  H  S  R  H  B  P  C  N  I  W  C  K  M  A  K  S  J  C  D  N  Y
              D  S  F  M  Q  H  S  E  B  T  H  I  P  Q  Z  Y  E  I  R  E  P  X  B  H  L  N  O  E  P  I  L  X
              R  C  N  P  E  Z  I  S  I  H  C  E  J  O  A  C  D  R  O  A  V  A  D  M  W  F  E  R  Q  K  M
              E  O  L  H  B  F  K  U  V  F  Q  K  N  L  X  F  C  D  J  T  C  W  G  T  P  I  G  O  H  O  W
              F  C  A  D  J  I  L  X  D  G  T  M  W  E  H  L  P  N  Q  N  E  N  V  W  B  F  Q  P  V
                    U  L  V  G  I  E  X  D  U  H  A  O  F  C  U  R  T  G
                    J  Q  K  D  L  G  T  U  T  D  S  Z  H
                    C  W  M  P  N  M  P  S  E  T  F  U
                    K  R  A  T  I  F  L  T  A  O  R
                    B  U  C  R  Q  M  I  D  G  E  Q
                    T  S  M  L  E  J  R  K  S  N  P
                    L  A  V  B  S
```

ASIA

(word search puzzle grid)

AFGHANISTAN

(word search puzzle grid)

CHINA

```
                              S T
                    L V U M        P        K
                    (I)S L N V R F D L U
                    L(A)K H A N D O Q
                    V I H M S G R(T)F
                    W J U B G T C A X E Y
                      D B N I A P Z G
                      R E W A F J H
                    L F E A K E H M I
                  (M O N S O O N S)
                    A L U M F P E Q N
            K T P J I M D
            G L P I N C N
            R A B O B O
        S A Z X W E I
(E Z T G N A Y)L M S W        B I G T Y F E V J
P Z X O R N(T H I R D)P K C I N Q W B  S H T C L J U D K M D A
A Y Q B P W R V U T C N V J M R H U A T I R S I Q A O E C W B
  P H V P G Z F O A I E L A D L U T S D T K U I O N E R P B N F E G
J Q I U O A F Y M H Q P Z Q K N P M(M A D S E G R O G E E R H T)A J N M Q O
R K T N P M X J I P L T U A O R L Y C H Q O P T P U H C F P E I E O Z S B P T
S W M E A S K L G N R S M L K S Z X I A N V E P A P D B Q C D V K L H Y R N A
L(R E V I R S U D N I)T U A I W S T U L A H Q N V Y G E D U X C Z U C A
  B O C N M J L N J Y V T M V O S M L R S D E A Y B E N H K T A H P V I J
  V A K F C K K U F C I B I W R X P E I T E W V A N O Q R S O N G W E D K
  T C T B Q A I S M B X E A J O Y Q K J U G P F Z P H X R Z T N U U M W L C
  A F O E T M L R M C D A G N Z N W A V I X R B G M(G O N G H E G U O)X D B
  D G O N H T(N O R T H E R N C H I N E S E)A Z H V R I H V U V H M F E
    P U Q E D C W K M H        Y J A Z K S G P I L F E I A J W T Y G A
    J F V I H K G L        H G L S Y(I H C I A T)K Z S X Z J
                        F B M I H X K Y B F H B L Y R I
                        O N E O W J S V E D C O M Q
                        P C R N I K T U C D G N P
                        Q S U V
                        T D
```

INDIA

```
                    T L C
              O M U V L
              K(I R A S)
              (K)H R
              E A G A
              M N F B
          D J C C O S P T
          C A I K H V Q U M                              L
          J T T H N E W T S                        U V Y O
(I H L E D W E N)R S X I Y                        A X L E
  G N K M L B N J O A S H R Z O        P V Y X     S R I P
  K C D K T S Q U P A C D N K P V Y X      (M U M B A I)
  I J F I R M E N F M T D S V(S E G N A G)I      B Q K
(T A R A H B U)A D F G B E D U R Q Z N W G W H U      Z L
  C H D I V H G N E A(C I L B U P E R)A T O V J W
  O I F    S C C P R L K F C A F R S K I S N Y G K
        W E J C S A U G B(H I M A L A Y A S)F H
        K G S B Z T D P E M H L Q D A E N J Z
        M A L R Y I H A E N P O C W Q M K O
        E U A W V U J N O E U B L R L P N
        X G Q X(D N O C E S)V I T I S
        N N Z P Z H Y H X W A Y A I
        Y A P O I P G A X R U Z
        O L B S A Q O T N L M
        J C T R F Z A X
      (D H O T I)I N
        K S F E D W T
        T D F N N O R
        L I V W U A
        U C M A E
        X E O V C
        S L U
        M
```

ISRAEL

IRAQ

IRAN

JAPAN

KOREA

MALAYSIA

SAUDI ARABIA

```
            A
            B C F
            K D M L
I O N H K G S L E O S T U
T P J Q C R J M N U X P W
A S B Q B D Z A E Y G V A L
T L R K I Z R J B E I D H K T
V U P O S C G Y F A V C U B S
M B W N H X V A B G L H U L K V
C N I Y A W C I M A L S I X J W
J H D K R C U A N O M T A Y B R
O G M L X Z S D F P S B Z W I U C
F P E Q Y T E Q A R H A H O D B T E
  M S L P C K F J A N I C G S A F U R Z L
  W V A O G B Q E O M G V W Q L T D J H K P
  R N T R X H A D P B H X M Y K J C I S P M T
  U Q X K A S R I T L V D R X H B H A O K S L
  Y O Z C G B J S K U W T A Z A G R Q D N V U
  P L C U V K I N G S A U D Y L E Y W Z R B G C
U L E K X T J S C O I P K N T I E X A F P E D H
V M W B Y M Z N R A Q D J E N I R H E Q R F T W V
O S N C R T N A J V L F M L L B O A P Z G Y S X U
C M T K F C M K W U J I K H A T A J H S C V U M L
O F N Z D L I X B E A G I C U V K B P S X W H T
  P E A S Y C T J K M D N R K Q J E S R O H F A
  Q J J B Z H I D B U I O A I P T R P E S C K G H
  G R E A G H R L A Q P J N S R O Q F T D U C B T J
  E C H D T C S S N L H K U O H N A U V C L M E B A
  D F V U D M L M A Z Y A L T G M B C Q W V H O R C
  Z Y W M U A G O P X B E U L F N A V K A L N Q I K
    X L K F R H F S A U D I R I Y A L H J M P B S D J L C
  A S V H C S Q B E M C K V M E L K S C R B E U A H D B F G C
  T U   D S W C T V E B X W D G K J I T W X L Z Q C A J E T L H
              U D G D J Y C T H F E V D Y P P D F S T S H F V
                I U Z A   U T M X U O G M C I V J X W
                  F         C T L H U X W M T
```

TAIWAN

```
                        F K
                      S D L M U
                  G C N I T A I J L
                P E A R L A S K B M
                  F L M H P I U O N
                U S C P Q D P N C B
                  I R W H Y Z E M C S
              U Q V X O A W I O E U
            F I U S P R T K D O M L
          D Z R I R J A D E G N H
        B L E U L T I M L E K L I
        R M A W O W S O F A J A M
          C E G N A G G N O D C K
        G A F P N I Q U K Q S N E
      M H K E D A X V P E T C R V
      A B J O J P R W A Y O Q U P
    L N I L K D Z X C I N Y X W
    C D L M O A Y J K S P Z D A
  V U A N I L P I L T H Y E O C
  B R R E P U B L I C A Q K I D
  N Q I F H B H T U M G O E S K
  R T N D C G U R N M R F I B
  O P C G F T Q O E A H U O J
S Z W H E I P T P T O S T A D
A X O I O Q G N I T N E K E K
  D Z N R F U V C C B F M J
  Y A E G S T X O Q A O H
  L B S E Z W Y F Z C U M
    E E O D I C C R F D
    H N R E T N A L S
    C L I G N T N B
      F K M I P C A
        J C O R E
        Q T S R
          U X V
            Z W
            Q U
            T I
```

TURKEY

```
                              S F
                            M L U A K
                            D S T B
                              H J
                      C V
                      U M L
                    C L T E M                X
                  A H M U W O V G F N O
            J     I G R N B U H E Y P M Y
            K B O K O J N J I D R Q V H T S R L Q
            L C P Q P A I T A C Z I L G U S H K B F C E
            S E A V A L K A B T K M R Z R I I C D A O V U
            D R F W M E N R B L S Z X J A S S J S B N W T
            T E U C Z B O A M A N I K F I N H T D M A F S N
              D I T E Y I R U H M U C E Y I K R U T G R O X
              Y F X Q H A W X O F R Q E K E A U E Y M Q Y L
              S E V P G R T Y V D I J A P W B I R Z M A Z M K N
                L T   U R Q P R Y S V L D A S I A M I N O R X W
                      Z E I C A I O Z Y B V G F R H P Q P O V Y K L
                      S P T U D T B M A H K H X S B O S J U B P E A M
                      A I S L A M I C B C G W G Q I C R T O Z O J F O G O L K
                    G B F K U C D A R D A N E L L E S R Q R B N S P I W R A L
                    V H W N B C K V I W T J D P I G A C D N U R G A M J Q N
                      D L J F U P K L O U S B U I F L A M I N G O S C
                        E M Y X F R W B C H U R M L H R T U P B M
                        O Z U M C L G T E V L J C F O I S I K T
              N       S A E B I F D H W K A A I E O M C M L
                    D C H S I K R U T D U C T V K A B
                    E F G X U Y Z X N N P H D I J
                      S L   O A W A V E F A K U
                            B S C O I E O I
                                  G R T
                                    H O
                                    V
```

VIETNAM

```
                  A T C S U
                  J K H L M V
        G     A M S N R O T N E M D L
        H O C H I M I N H C I T Y O P V
          L F B E H O V U M F D R C Q
        K T S I N U M M O C K S U
          C I D P O W X N H N B T
          J O   Y G Z A I G
              H G N A N J
                A O N A
                L I A O
        G N A N A D
        Z H X W V   A I
                  A   U E
                  M   T
                  I   N
                  A   L
                  L M H
                  H R G
                  S E R
                  V E U
                  E Z M T
                  N T Z X I
                  D R U O A
                  G H G L F
                  E B E J K
                  H A R M E L
                  I A C M E A F
                  I D B O L A N
                  T O P S N S I
                  N A G M S P
                  R L Q A I A
                  O N S P P N
                  O I T C A
                  N U M B R
                X L V B I F M D
                Y A W A C E H E
                K Z J Y I G L
              J A C Y C L O N
              V C E L P Q
        R U N K E Q
        K I T E S R
        Z C T Y Y W S
          A E T Z Y X
          A B K
          E D
          D
```

116

AUSTRALIA

EUROPE

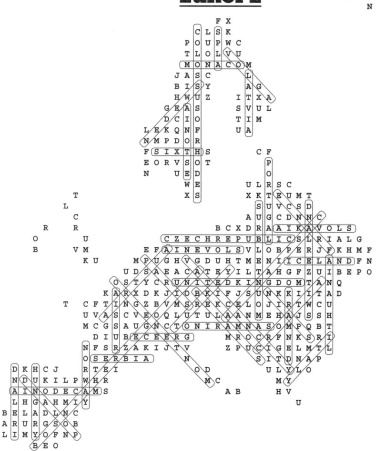

GERMANY

CZECH REPUBLIC

FRANCE

IRELAND

ITALY

POLAND

```
                              T
                        L M X C
                    B I A J Y H V
                F O L E M F W A G B        D R A V F Y G E H T U X O
            V Q G P N I C T K I H D V U F L C S K U B C F H G H B G A
        R Z N T W U L B T A X E D F H R C T E A Q Z A E Z L D R J I K L N
        P A R O B M U K H U H Y Q D E D A U A B T G T Z X K J A V F C P O
        Y X S Z T R W C A J S P W I T S W I E T O K R Z Y S K I E R G M N
        Q V R Z E Y V X T E I R D H F X W E N D F Y A G H M S L E D S T Z O
        A W Y K S C Y A B Z L N Z C I A Y C P S U B T L V T A R G W E V M U
        E U X D I V Z C X D O T S J S T B E M F O X S D U B C O H F O D L C
        C Z S F A U R Y S Y P E A K G Z E L D A B J H L K N G A X I Y P Q S T
        T B D G N W L U P V U M U K R H L T G Z V C A B V A T D J Z R S B U
        N H O O T B C B O W A W L S A O E A Y N W R I J O B F K X D W V
        S P M L X M G E F S L V D H F V C X I C V U C U G U C Y L Z A
        L O U O S D T B E T P N M G Z E A H Q L C J L W T N A E H J C
        R I A P P A L C H S A O B O T Z L O T Y E Q K A P U I T D B K U W
        K T V Q E B D A D L B K L T N H E Z N W U D B R V F N P G Y L X V
        Q W B R O C X Z W E Y X N I Y S B W I D B X E S L A B M M A M R Y
        I X N F L A O J R C J A J T K K J Y W T R M A Q W F E P A Z K L
        J A G I E L L O N I A N P X A C V O M A P O W G X U O Q T C M B
        Y Z H M J A I K C G Z O K H Y P K X Z W C N T X L S R B J S R O
        C I L K K L M O D I Z O W A D O E O D U A I R Y E E I C Q A J E
        J K D E E H B E A F P L V U H P L F L E P H Z M I K H U T P N F
        F H S N O B D H R Y I T A I U S I O Q S A B T F C V K G L A M
        G A P F E Q V M L E N O W L K K U G T U G I W D H D I Z N
        I       C G U S J O S C L Q O Z A K Z C I L E I W D B O C
        S       T W N K S Z V M G E H T F S B Y X F E Q P Y
                X I P F A R U K H N B R U T A Z R C H X
                R I O N H Y L T P C X A S I G W
                H G T S J F M E V H L T U B V
                Q J    P X G R A C W Z R K J L
                   I       Q          M O Z
                                          N
```

ROMANIA

```
                              T X O
                        V C N A M A L U
                    B U T J X O I S C    A R M T I W H I Z W
                A P T M U W P N L N U T P O S B V X O H G D E
            R L O S K A I O K M X D S Q N L U K C J C X F O P
            Q O U L E V K Y I S A N A P A P M U L X A E K U A
            N Z N M R V B L Q J N B V R H I M T X A C L E J T V W
            F S A B M J Z H N U W A E T J N E C J H A A E S B A X I
            M Y P J T K C M B P H W M S P A L T Q M F W L I R C K J
        G T E U S Q W D E Z Q R L U H Q M N U R P G H C M I L Y B O
        L E O U R M N I T G I G M O X J R O K A V O Q D N L H Z M E P
        F K J F R B A P U E L N A I N A M O R S S L T S Q B G B Q N C W
        G U H G D O C J X Y N I M S T R K U A O H K A L U C A R D V E X
        B L R D Q P V D M O H U D M U F A O R M C D R G T P F P F E U D U R
        A S M K T E I R O D L A E F A T S Q P U L I C L U E O E M E V T I S C
        O Q P Z A N O A G A I N X O L E U N B Z X L E T R P F B G F A E Q B D T
        J C H D R P C K B S V I V R V A R U C U B P Q G E A N K T L K R A Y X
        N V X H E N E F B G D A B Y D M L T V U B X Q Z D O U J M P I U W Q S    C E O
        I A Z S S B A J H P W E N U X J K H S P F V R C V C H A S N O Z T U A Q M B T U D
        O Y W J T I D C D Z U P K O W A C B A E Q P H U W M B E A R S C A V E A U S    R X
        B I R W L F A E V Q C O G Q D F I R R U S X B D I V K N W B Z C R S T    Z
        X K E X E I G A E P J I Z B D A H A Z A Y T E L L Q J V F X E S I P M
        C A E L G F E C Q R L T M E X U B S Y R H I K Y R P I C G E T L T O U
        T M K H Z F U A D A I T E V G G R O J C S A S H L Z Y S E K A L J
        U B M O U N T M O L D O V E A N U T O D M U D B R U Z Y O
        A T A T S I L I E P U C X T N A M X B F N T A C H V N K X B
        X M D R C E T T O E H J U H R U A Y V G E    M W A L E
        A U S W E X G U F W T M O Z Q E
        S T F U I Z M J D I K C B T
        B G H T U K L E J V L
```

RUSSIA

J
I Z K
R N L
K H E T M
G O R U M L
S F W A S T K H
X R Q E L B U R S A
W K H C B T C R Q L Q U
R C L I F E V T U Q S E T P C
E T B E Y B U A L R Q S F E S P D P A S I D F
X R U S F K T S B J Y N R U S S I A N P D S W O E U D S B X Z T S
R E P U B L I C U K C P W Q Z I X D C A E H K G R U X G R A O T U E C O
T U D C A L J A R A R X V Y H N A N T H T Q T I O M E T D F O U W R D
A M B D B G M S V E I O A G R G C W S F E C P R A N C L V H A Y E N B A
S U B O T A N I P G L D U Z J I R M E U O L V J N K B H K Y W I M N X J L
C H G L S U H O I W Z H M T S A S L T P L O S T E C A F J B I C R Z K F E
A L C R C X T A O G E N F D J N F K A Q P K H M U T C Z I X J E A M L T
U R A L M O U N T A I N S E K Q N B S N D A L X E R I R X A B P M G I N Y D R
X I Z B H J W S X Y F K A M L B V O M R T Y R T N U O C T S E G R A L U C B T U
A Z O Q H E P Y D N C O P G U L X P A H A J S E P O I K A L H G O Z K H G F
R B D A N I L M E R K L T M H S K Q P E A S F M V A T U
U E T H I U S O C U I B S R N W Z T K M L
C R I T X U P Y G D C F U A U N O O
J Z V X A V L T M V T
W I

SLOVAKIA

T A U H V L M
F D I C A U H K W S F A G Z Y
R E G H C T I L J K M J I L G T H B V B X H Q
E P Q O E N B M V R P S Y K S V O H C A L R E G G M R O
P A S A H Y M U Z L E Z K I Y X V I O B Q B Y W O R U N
T U R V X O N O V S Y L H O Z V B A R S R P O C N R I L
Z V B A Y A C Z L U A T G M N G A F K R J O U V W O D T M
B U A L C C W K Q P K B X A I K A V O L S O H C E Z C O Z S
C I G J S W Y S I H A B E E K R W H E R N C W E K L N T U E K J B L A
T H U V K N I E K U R U Y T V U C C A O D F D I M L U E
D R P A R T I N A T C O D S J A D V E P E T I
S E Q L A K X O F E O V R E R I C U S R Q N U
P K R E M N I C A M I N T S H R S G
B Z M E K J B H E F A G
O N Y T A E I P D T
G O U L A S H
V M Q P O

SPAIN

A
C I O H
M K Z R Y L N
F B D U G J O P Z A K
P Y R E N E E S L F P Q U
X S B U I H Q G M J V A E T
E T Y R V S N E B W R D F S I L M
W L A O I A X B R J H R Q O T
L C B K Y C Z A G K S N P U V
U D S R E V I R O R B E X F C E
B U A T I M U A C B T U V H R A F
X G E S H L W V L V H A I B C K Z D S J A
F D J H I R J M K I X G D R C A N A R Y A X U F T
Q L C T R O X V H Z U S U Z T S S L M C N M A K H B
O E M P F Y W A U Q S P Q F D S T U Q Y R Z I I P U R M V
P A S E O V J F M U M S O L W C I S X U V A T A L L E A P U L
I N Z G Y G C H K L A R N T B A V L C B P E N S L Q A D C X
X V H F H P N P D B E V D G A F E D I A Q O R S F O M H
U W P A R L I A M E N T A R Y M O N A R C H Y I U
J G Z I L C N C W G X I C H I R U T N U U N G S
A T V E T A M N Y O W J E Q E R D I C S B G H T
Q K J Y S H T U V I D L K B D F C D J P M T V
L F Z S I A U R Z U O E P A S H Z H K A I
P S B O K B G N S H N W I T L G I Q B E N W
R O M A D O C N E M A L F X Y E D J G P G I X
B O N L S H O R G F S J A A I L T F L S B
N E M T C F U B A T R Z C R U D A L Y H I
C G R I B E R I A N K M I L V E M Z E
P Q U D J P B R E L Q O C W I O A O
D V W K E Q C D O Q M N X Z J
X P S N Y K N

UNITED KINGDOM

SWEDEN

SWITZERLAND

NORTH AMERICA

CANADA

COSTA RICA

```
L
U O V T
M R N S N M H     S G
K C R H A F K J P A E T U U A P
I G L C I B K Q T E R A Q O R
U E M O L C S R O A U N G E H M I Z R J N
G C N H A O T B I Q Y A C R B N L A Q S U M K
D I W V B Z U V C H X V C N F K D K J P B T I L O
Y X Y E P R A Y D S C W O A C M S I C I L O H T A C P
B Z C F M D L X E G F A S Z S M D J H Y O C W V H Q R W
R E P U B L I C A D E C O S T A R I C A X M T X G A V X E
G H K J H Q   P F A P E L E C R Q P A O U C Y T R I H
A L N S R P   X D C T E S A O W M N L C R Z C S D G R
O M I T W V   B R K B D E A S E O V F T I E K J S U
U L K H N   E F T Z L D A O F K E U L H P L Q L T
M J I   E J U E P R N O L O C T B E S O D A S V
O   V G S Y R U J A G J E A U C S N O N X A W
I W H X U V O T R E D G P I M A P E I Y Z
P S S H B G T N E D I S E R P
E A Z C O B R J G B A A I
I B E P C B F Z H P O
F E I K U Q C N J
D T R E D M S L
A L R S R T K
R H S I N A P S T
C M X W H B V U
O A Y Z B C E
M   A C D F
O E N   T U L
D Z R   Z X
R
```

DOMINICAN REPUBLIC

```
A U P   P U T D
Q N Z T Z G E M V S E
S M R U H A I E S C F T U J
K B P R I M E R O D E M A Y O Q A O B
L A V W Y B E E W G G T V K N P Q R E
K T E X C P C N S A N T I A G O E N A B
C Y P U S A G Q R H I W L M T S B C L C
J A B E B D U P B I X M D R O M T H D O N
Z L P Q T Z E A R T I B O N I T E E A E I
D I I X D C R R X A J Y N M D Z C L S F M A N O
C A G Q N O T A O K Q L Z I P O V U G H C K C A B R E H T A E L
A H H E M T J Y U L E E D N Y X T K Z I K Q P U P V C W D A O H P
T B T R W I L K X D M C A I R E D N L E L L A B E S A B P N I R E Q
G H K H L F C U M E Z P G F C S W F B A I J R T S A Z I Y X E G N S Z Y T
E S E C O N D A V U N O N B H A N A U G I S O R E C O N I H R J L I O S U M
F K D C U V G P Q T N E D I S E R P Q J Y   B   K F M X U T L
R H S I N A P S W Y   T E V I W   W V
A I E U Y R   R U H X
L G J O H R
H D K T J O
F P N S I T
L M Z K
E Q U
R
```

MEXICO

```
B D L
P   A
C   H
K   T F E F D   U M
U L E S P A N I S H
U   B M K T L R V L X C
O   H R E T A W E M I L
H   C S G C D W Q A M O   U A
J X   F U X T O B R N P L T V N
P   K M A M U S U M A C I N T A
L   H L C Z E U P S Z E W O M F
U   B T X A D O N A Y X D N L N
T   U I F N C K I C J H I G O
G J H B L B D I K O P C D P
S O Y A M E D O C N I C I G I
F   O U T Y S R Q S L C F A O
M V Z T X Y B E O J D H
B A W I U W K D L E M N
T R C P C L X E F L U G
D B E V N O M O Q O P T
R O R U Y C R B S G N
P S T O Z I I R M F E        O H L M
Q C R E A H J Z X U H D I    Y G K N
D F B G J U A R E Z I E      J Q R I
K V U T B S R M S J K        V F S
W X A Z T B E D L P        E U T W
Y R I O G R A N D E Q V B X A D
A S C P M O P U S R W Y J
N S N A E B O A C A C
T S   Z C B
```

NICARAGUA

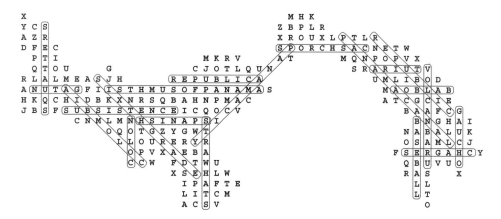

PANAMA

PUERTO RICO

UNITED STATES OF AMERICA

SOUTH AMERICA

ARGENTINA

P L Z X
B F A C B Y C
D K H T H G I E O
P L T S A A F E C B H A
A H G P R O G A Q R S D
C N D K E P N O D F A S
I M J L P A C T N T P
S L L A F U C A U G I M T L M P
L B T K G B N M C S E A R O Q
F U C H P L B A F L R P G B
Q P N O K I J I Z E R N H
M E R L T C S Z P G A D C
P B R W U V R U H O T D F A
X M A T E P L A N T E B K
D H Y C Y B D G C E L A
A S C E O A N B H M F B
Z I K G I N O H O L U N
E N A G A U C H O E E U P S
O A F U J K E A N S G R E Q
M X P W F H V S O G T O D H I
C B S E P G S S U K U N I A
D A Y C O A U Z A A
Z O Q O I N Y L
U R C V R W A M X
A T I E D B
D S S C O K
S N A M B J
U E L D A L I
P C Q O H
F R S G R
D E C S
P P T
E U B
F S U O N
V I A P M
W T H Z
G X U Y L
I O
J G
A K

BRAZIL

A
I P K M B
F O B L Q Z O M D C R P
S T E S H N O M J R S R N Z N A L V
T U M U C U M A Q U E P L E Z B O Q W
I G Y U D L C J I P L A Q I A K C R Z W S Y
L X L Y M V B K U H I K L B J A U A X F A E C
T W F A W X C B G O B W Y F C T S Y P H G Z X B I P O Q
A G Z S E L E V F L N S A O F R A N C I S C O L D H A O S R F L
H D S N A I D N I E G P O M B G D I A L A H N E M K J T P I R K G
R Q B O E N K V C F N F D I O J X Z E N B L R V W I E U I R E E F F O C
C P R T J U Z D T L R Y X T R A X F M K O I B W A R C S B N J I M H N
I S A M H E T A S U Y W I O M A K S C Z X O A A R A B Y P A C
G U W E C A I H B L J N P T Y U D X J T B J Q P D O
V R S F I V W G H I J B T D A Y W U I A E C F E
D T C L A R G E S T H N P Z V K R F D O G
K J H L N M I C A E S E U G U T R O P
G U V U O B N I B R Q O T U L S T I U
T M Z P O L D E B T N M V B W R X
S A C I Q H D H S V U A Z J Y I
N T M N H E R E P U B L I C A K
Q O A Q X G F E L Z L A O N H L
E P D P G S X M R C B P A G M
R R Y I A T E V U D M F R Q
F S T O L R A S T E S X
A Z P C V U M T
W U A H A
O U B
U L K
M W O C
V T I R
P L H Z
K

COLOMBIA

C
F
L H
O M
L C F S K
R A M U A E
X G V N U P
E U T F A
O A G K L
J H M D C B M X N
C I A W E Q P A Y Z A
A R V R P F D N O B E
H T U S E A G R D C L W
M I A T I O Q N S X E G U V
L K J L N P R E Y T A V Z Q Y I W V N U
O C E A N S L X E N D I L X R Z M Q T O
A F Y G T U A Y A C G P R S A V S R I P A L H B G D
N I A H B Y P W E O Q L I O N M A R M O S E T F M
L E T M S R Z J K N B S T R C U Q V P C O J N C E
O C R K A E V F B D N E V A D O D E L R U I Z W X
K J I H R C G I L O C N B Q U A N T U Z X M C Y N
D P A Q S C I D M R G M P S M T S I Z Y W L B O V
F N P H O E L K N Q O E E A R F K R V K T L I U M
H A G I S N J B M L D T N I L J R G O I O H J A
P N E B O Z M R A U E Q U A T O R E A F C O F F E E
R I Q O V A R C A M O P L C L E B K P G L E B K C L D
S T S R C Y U E B L P D E Q E G K L U A H
U H A R E C E D A M L A P C R R L F M T B N M
Y E V D M H K F N C V S B E D J C N S O L I
Z X A U W I X D A X W Z Q F L E Y U T Q I Q
L O D T G H U Y T A H I O C S P R C O
S G O R G O N A I S L A N D
L B G Q R B S T C F J
M N F C H F P L O K A Z
O P L U T D Y A U T S
V M W U T C N F B K
E X K F A L D O M
Q O P N
C

ECUADOR

A E
O W K X A
L H P N B I B C N D K F
Q J D R M V C L Q Y M L R J
K I G C O B G Z O G I E C S G O
T E S T F W N P H V U D T F C B T U Q N L P K
F U O X C A I R T A P O E V L A S F S M H Z J A
E P D Y P Z R W Q O Y R Q E A S E V R P Y I S M N
F A C I L B U P E R U S P U G R C W T U W A D L B Q
O L X S I Q A H R S X V O I Z I D Y X D V S X N N M R O P
N I K C K T J E D L N E U D T N H B G U A Y A Q U I L T
G M J E L Y P T M O T F Q K C O J Z Q G E L E C U N S S
P R Q R Z U X N J G O M O B O C C K H F S D E X V D J H
Y Q X I P O B H G E R Q I W N H F T I A P I Z Y Q W H O M K
A H A O L L I A W I H A P N A V D I W O S S A R U C O I L
Z W H I A U J F R S L X W K S U A B O J O I F A Q P N
R G C P T K V T O U W Y M L H L L G K B T A S T R Q
B V C H I M B O R A Z O V O L C A N O U N B E O B
F S O M T C U Q V B A G S J T P N B V C G D A R
K U C N U B H W T Z N I U R A E D X L W M Y Z
E I D L D T I A H D F Q L C U E N C A X
T J X C N Z E Y A K F D S A
C V L C S G P V C G
T D M D S H C W B O
Y R O K C I A A L X
E A N V N G X Y N
Z P L J C A H E M
Q R L H O G L W Z
F I O L H N A D
S N D U K B N V
G A T S M I F D C
H U J C P T U
Q D A
E B S
R

VENEZUELA

A
J M K V
B Q N R L I B S U
M K L C U A T R O W X K J
O J P O K H R L E I T M Z D C O P V G F H P L
P C T S E C I Y S A K Y I R A V I L O B D A D U I C I
N I J N D R V J D R A X H B N R U M D H R Q E N N O Q X S E U
Q G D Y A W G B A I Q L O L C M T Q A E F G I P S A I M B W C T D
H R S C I L B U P E R V P H R W R S L R L C N C S A O D Z A Y R F V
F E Z L X I V Z U F O I M I M O G L O R I A A L B R A V O P U E B L O B H
A U E W A Y G E U Z N L N P R O C C K L H S J O A A O G M S O P A C Z
H B V D U X A F E G A F O U V K J E J O K B K A H C G N L L E S I J
T C F C L A I P R U T R C B N E I P Q C D A N N C K I U I U R F D Y
D T B O Q O T O F D A I P F G C T A B H V A T A Q X
C E J R E S P G C H R B S E U L M U J A F V N P W G
F W I I H L M A U U G R A C G O E H
D O P F T A N C V I C D W Q P R Y
C B L A K E M A R A C A I B O N A K V
A X L T G C G B N X L B Z X H Q N U P L
Z Y L F A U I H A T W A L Y I R M T O M
S K J M F N Z Y Y J Z A K L S R
Q L G I V E F I H
I M R E V J K S
H Y A W E E I L D
P O N P X L X T P W
V R X D T Z Q R N
W U C H T A S M V O X
T H S I N A P S
S Y A L B T U
B Z C D